Building Progressive Web Applications with Vue.js

Reliable, Fast, and Engaging Apps with Vue.js

Carlos Rojas

Apress®

Building Progressive Web Applications with Vue.js: Reliable, Fast, and Engaging Apps with Vue.js

Carlos Rojas
Medellin, Colombia

ISBN-13 (pbk): 978-1-4842-5333-5   ISBN-13 (electronic): 978-1-4842-5334-2
https://doi.org/10.1007/978-1-4842-5334-2

Managing Director, Apress Media LLC: Welmoed Spahr
Acquisitions Editor: Spandana Chatterjee
Development Editor: Matthew Moodie
Coordinating Editor: Shrikant Vishwakarma

Cover designed by eStudioCalamar

Cover image designed by Pixabay

Distributed to the book trade worldwide by Springer Science+Business Media New York, 233 Spring Street, 6th Floor, New York, NY 10013. Phone 1-800-SPRINGER, fax (201) 348-4505, e-mail orders-ny@springer-sbm.com, or visit www.springeronline.com. Apress Media, LLC is a California LLC and the sole member (owner) is Springer Science + Business Media Finance Inc (SSBM Finance Inc). SSBM Finance Inc is a **Delaware** corporation.

For information on translations, please e-mail rights@apress.com, or visit http://www.apress.com/rights-permissions.

Apress titles may be purchased in bulk for academic, corporate, or promotional use. eBook versions and licenses are also available for most titles. For more information, reference our Print and eBook Bulk Sales web page at http://www.apress.com/bulk-sales.

Any source code or other supplementary material referenced by the author in this book is available to readers on GitHub via the book's product page, located at www.apress.com/978-1-4842-5333-5. For more detailed information, please visit http://www.apress.com/source-code.

Printed on acid-free paper

To my grandmothers, who always believed in me . . .

Table of Contents

About the Author

 **Carlos Rojas** is an engineer with more than ten years of experience building digital products. He is focused on front-end technologies (HTML, CSS, JS, Angular, and Vue.js) and mainly edge web technologies such as web components and progressive web apps. He also has some experience working with fast-changing business environments such as startups. Carlos enjoys sharing knowledge during talks in meetups, and helping startups and companies to run workflows to make excellent digital products. As a result of this, his books convey the love he has for the construction of scalable, high-quality products.

About the Technical Reviewer

Yogendra Sharma is a developer with experience in architecture, design, and development of scalable, distributed applications, with a core interest in microservices and Spring. He currently works as an Internet of things (IoT) and cloud architect at Intelizign Engineering Services in Pune, India. He also has hands-on experience in technologies such as AWS, IoT, Python, J2SE, J2EE, Node.js, Vue.js, Angular, MongoDB, and Docker. Yogendra constantly explores technical novelties, and he is open-minded and eager to learn about new technologies and frameworks. He has reviewed several books and video courses published by Packt.

Acknowledgments

To my friends, because they always found time to review my code and drafts.
To my colleagues, because they helped me a lot with their feedback.
To Yogendra, because his attention to detail made this a better book.
To my editors, because their feedback and reviews made this book a
high-quality guide.

Introduction

Progressive web apps (PWAs) were initially introduced by Google in 2015 and proved to bring many advantages to the web platform. In this book, we are going to examine how to empower our web apps to be fast and reliable, and to provide an immersive user experience with offline support.

In Chapter 1, we create our first PWA. I guide you in all the steps you need to know to add offline capabilities and to make a simple web app a PWA. In Chapter 2, we take a look at the web app manifest, which is a simple, but powerful, specification that allows the browsers when can install a web app like a native app according to the operating system. In Chapter 3, we study service workers, which are an amazing mechanism to handle background events with JavaScript. In Chapter 4, we examine cache storage and good-practice workflows to keep our offline data updated. In Chapter 5, we look at the main features and advantages of using Vue.js, a modern JavaScript framework. In Chapter 6, we study how to use a database supported widely in modern browsers, called *IndexedDB*, and how we can take advantage of its asynchronous capabilities to empower our PWAs. In Chapter 7, we look at a simple, but powerful, application programming interface, called *Background Sync*, that will allow our app to make the user experience easy. In Chapter 8, we improve our engagement with our app and examine how to add push notifications to it. Last, in Chapter 9, we polish the details of our app and make it available to the world.

CHAPTER 1

Making Your First Progressive Web App

Welcome to this journey of building your first progressive web app (PWA). In this chapter, we build VueNoteApp, which is a simple notebook app, and then convert it to a PWA, all while discovering some critical concepts along the way.

What Is a PWA?

PWAs are a trend that points to where web development is evolving. Therefore, it is essential to be exposed to this technology and spend some time studying it.

PWAs are the intersection between a web interaction and a mobile app user experience. Some of the features you'll find in PWAs are as follows[1]:

- *Progressive*: They work for every user.

- *Adaptable*: Their functionality adapts to the device regardless of whether it is a mobile, desktop, tablet, and so on.

---

[1]Pete LePage, "Your First Progressive Web App," `https://developers.google.com/web/fundamentals/codelabs/your-first-pwapp/`, n.d.

© Carlos Rojas 2020
C. Rojas, *Building Progressive Web Applications with Vue.js*,
https://doi.org/10.1007/978-1-4842-5334-2_1

- *Connectivity independent*: They support offline functions, in addition to low-quality connections or LiFi.

- *App style*: For users, PWAs are similar to a downloadable app from a store.

- *Fresh*: Thanks to their caching strategies, they are updated every time a connection is available.

- *Secure*: They work with HTTPS.

- *Discoverable*: Search engines are capable of indexing PWAs and detecting them as apps.

- *Able to be reengaged*: They allow push notifications after users install them, similar to apps you download from a store.

- *Installable*: They allow users to have the app available on their device with an access icon, just like apps that download from a store.

- *Linkable*: They can be shared easily with a URL.

To become familiar with the power of PWAs, check out `https://pwa.rocks/`.

Why Build a PWA?

PWAs open a new universe of possibilities to extend capabilities in web apps and provide users with a familiar experience. Some advantages in choosing to build PWAs instead of using other technologies are as follows:

- *Web platform*: Web capabilities are robust and extended in the major mobile and desktop operating systems.

- *Web developers*: Start in web developing is accessible and inclusive. All web technologies are open; you don't have software restrictions.

- *Distribution*: Web browsers are distribution channels. PWAs are shared easily with URLs.

- *Easy deployment*: You don't need to wait for approval of fixes or new features; just push your code to your server and, instantly, you have a new version.

- *Low friction*: App stores are a stressful experience for beginning users. With PWAs, you only need a link to install them.

What Is the Structure of a PWA?

Progressive applications are, in general terms, a regular Single Page Aplication. That is, they have the regular structure of a web app or single-page application (SPA), with an index (`index.html`) and HTML, Cascading Style Sheets (CSS), and JavaScript (JS) files. But, in addition to these items, three other things are required to be considered a PWA:

1. *A manifest file*: A file that describes the information in the PWA

2. *An app icon*: An image used as an icon on mobile devices when installed

3. *Service workers*: A JS file registered in the browser that allows tasks such caching and pushing notifications, among other things

So, this is what we are going to create next, after we go over some prerequisites.

Getting Started

To start to build our first PWA, we need to examine and install some technologies.

Node.js

Node.js is a JS runtime environment. Most of the projects using JS use Node to install dependencies and create scripts to automate the development workflow.

You install Node on your machine by downloading it from https://nodejs.org/en/.

After you download the installer, run it (Figure 1-1).

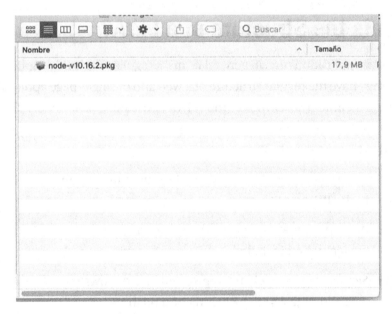

Figure 1-1. *Node.js installer package*

Follow the instructions. Figure 1-2 shows the welcome page.

Figure 1-2. *Installer step 1*

When this is complete, open your terminal and run

$node -v

If everything is okay, you'll see the Node version in your terminal (Figure 1-3).

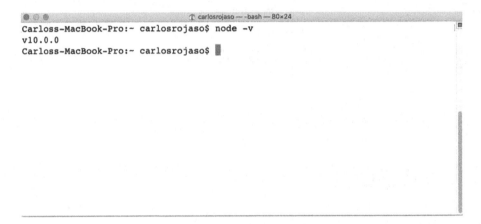

Figure 1-3. *Terminal node version command*

npm

When you install Node.js, you install npm, which is a package manager for JS. It is the default package manager for Node and it consists of a command-line client, called *npm*, and an online database of packages called the *npm registry*.

Check the version of npm you are running (Figure 1-4):

```
$npm -v
```

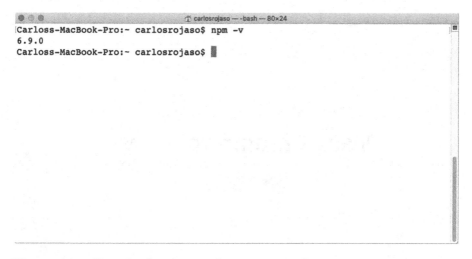

Figure 1-4. *Terminal npm version command*

Google Chrome

Chrome is a web browser that provides excellent support to PWAs and includes Chrome DevTools, which is a handy feature for developers. You can download and install from

```
https://www.google.com/chrome/
```

To install, just run the installer and follow the steps. The result is shown in Figure 1-5.

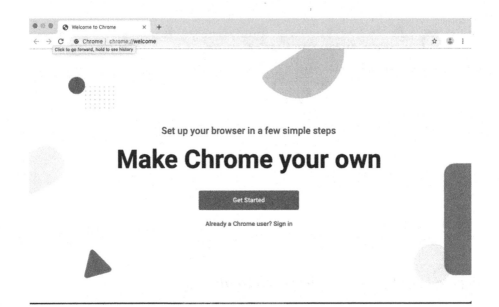

Figure 1-5. *Google Chrome installed*

Chrome DevTools

As mentioned, Chrome DevTools (Figure 1-6) is a set of web developer tools included in the Google Chrome browser. DevTools helps developers diagnose problems in their apps and makes their apps faster.

Figure 1-6. *Google Chrome DevTools*

Lighthouse

Lighthouse is an open source, automated tool for improving the quality
of web pages (Figure 1-7). By default, Chrome DevTools comes with
Lighthouse in the Audits tab. Learn more about Lighthouse at `https://`
`developers.google.com/web/tools/lighthouse/`.

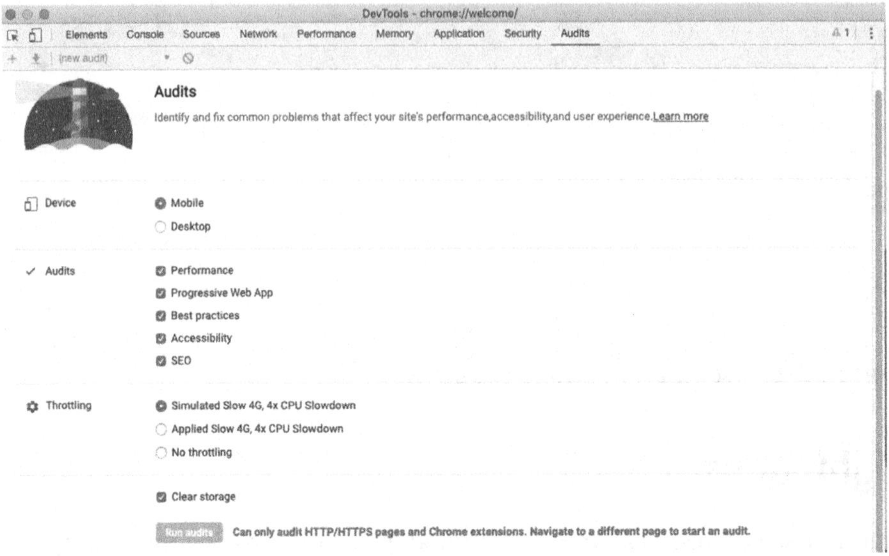

Figure 1-7. Google Chrome DevTools Audits tab

Vue

In the examples for each chapter in this book, we are going to use the Vue.
js framework. Vue.js is a straightforward and refreshing framework for
JS. Vue is oriented mainly in the view layer, but we can add what we need
and build powerful PWAs with all the tools that are part of its ecosystem.

Using Vue in projects is really easy. Add the following to `index.html`:

```
<!-- development version, includes helpful console warnings -->
<script src="https://cdn.jsdelivr.net/npm/vue/dist/vue.js">
</script>
```

or

```
<!-- production version, optimized for size and speed -->
<script src="https://cdn.jsdelivr.net/npm/vue"></script>
```

Vue CLI

Vue CLI is a full system for rapid Vue.js development. Thanks to Vue CLI, we can avoid extra work when dealing with Webpack, ESLint, and other tools, and just focus on building business logic in our apps. Install Vue CLI on your terminal:

```
$npm install -g @vue/cli
```

Material Design

Material Design is a visual language that synthesizes the timeless principles of good design with the innovation of technology and science. It is used on the Web and for Android devices. You can add Material Design to your web applications through libraries. These are some of the most popular:

- `https://getmdl.io/`
- `https://materializecss.com/`
- `https://www.muicss.com/`

For our project, we are going to use Vuetify because it is designed explicitly for Vue.

Vuetify

Vuetify is a semantic component framework for Vue. It aims to provide clean, semantic, reusable components that make building applications a breeze. To learn more about Vuetify, go to `https://github.com/vuetifyjs/vuetify#introduction`. Briefly, Vuetify is a collection of elements that allows you to apply Material Design guidelines to apps.

To use Vuetify in our project, we need to create a project in Vue using the Vue CLI. Inside the project, we need to run

```
$ vue add vuetify
```

Workbox

Workbox is a set of libraries and Node modules that make it easy to cache assets and take full advantage of features used to build PWAs. To learn more about Workbox, go to `https://developers.google.com/web/tools/workbox/`. You need to install it on your system:

```
$npm install workbox-cli --global
```

Firebase

Firebase is a service in the cloud that helps automate back-end developer tasks. Firebase is a place where you can save data and assets, and authenticate users without having back-end knowledge. Firebase is robust, and Google backs it. You need to install Firebase CLI on your terminal:

```
$npm install -g firebase-tools
```

In addition, you need to sign up:

```
https://firebase.google.com/
```

Now we need to create a new project. I created the project `appress-book-pwa`, where I connect all the features with our PWA (Figure 1-8).

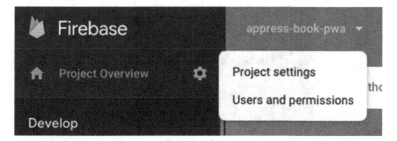

Figure 1-8. *Firebase web console project overview*

Firebase Hosting

Firebase Hosting is a hosting service where we can serve all our static files, connect our domain, and get a secure sockets layer (or SSL) certificate quickly with an easy deploy.

You can find Firebase Hosting in your web console (`https://console.firebase.google.com`) in Develop ➤ Hosting (Figure 1-9).

Figure 1-9. *Firebase web console hosting*

Firebase Database

Firebase Database is a service that allows us to add a remote database to keep our user data. In addition, it is an excellent option for handling real-time data in our app—meaning, we can open our app from a mobile device and a desktop, and we'll see the same information (Figure 1-10).

Figure 1-10. *Firebase web console database*

Firebase Cloud Messaging

Firebase Cloud Messaging is the service that allows us to send push notifications without having to deal with tricky server setups.

Git

Git is a version control system designed to handle the different changes in our projects. We will use Git to manage our web app project and handle the progressive steps we encounter in each chapter. You can download and install Git from

```
https://git-scm.com/downloads
```

Download the installer and run the wizard (Figure 1-11).

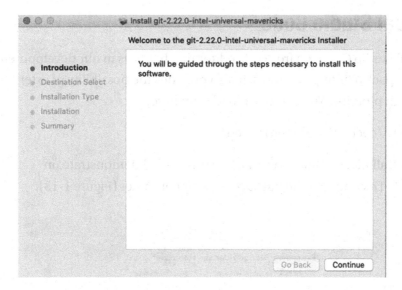

Figure 1-11. *Git installer step 1*

Follow the steps. An example is provided in Figure 1-12.

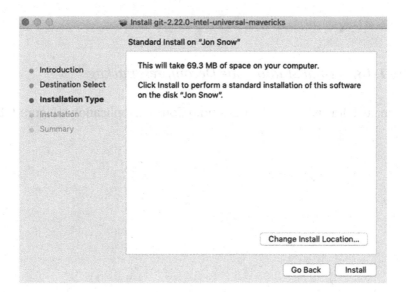

Figure 1-12. *Git installer step 3*

Visual Studio Code

Visual Studio Code is a free code editor that helps us in our development with a pack of integrated tools. It also provides the possibility of extending through plug-ins. You can download from here:

`https://code.visualstudio.com/`

Installation is simple on all platforms. Here I demonstrate on macOS. Decompress the package on your computer (Figure 1-13).

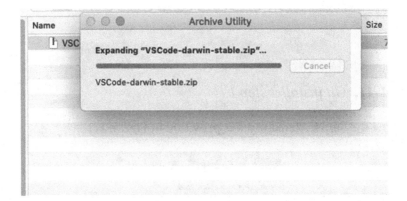

Figure 1-13. *Visual Studio Code Decompress package*

Then, just drag and drop Visual Studio Code to Applications (Figure 1-14).

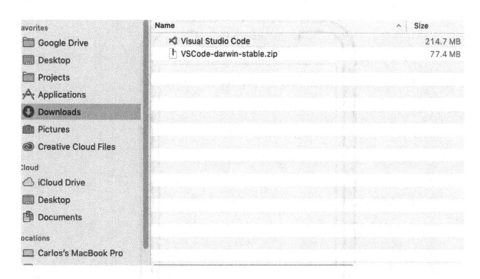

Figure 1-14. *Drag and drop Visual Studio Code to Applications*

You can find tons of code editors, but we use Visual Studio Code in this book mainly because it is free, it works smoothly, and it has a big plug-in ecosystem.

The App Shell Model

The App Shell Model includes the minimum required HTML, CSS, and JS needed to activate the user interface (UI). The cache is used to increase reliability of repeated visits. In this way, the app shell does not load from the network during every user visit; it does so from the cache. Only the critical content of the network is loaded—usually, the updated content.

In our app, we define our application shell as the header, background, and main button, which are loaded from the cache each time (Figure 1-15).

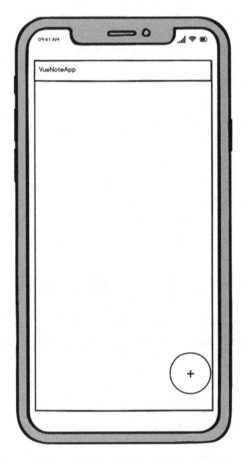

Figure 1-15. *App shell design in VueNoteApp*

Also, the content (Figure 1-16) includes the elements loaded dynamically from the network.

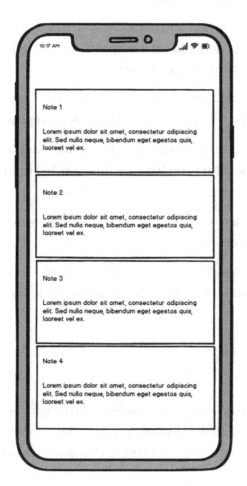

Figure 1-16. *Content element design in VueNoteApp*

We can think of the App Shell Model as the skeleton of our UI and the core components necessary to get our app off the ground. The benefits of an app shell architecture are as follows:

- *Fast performance*: Static HTML, CSS, and JS are cached on the first visit, so they load instantly on repeat visits.

- *App-like style*: We can create experiences with offline support similar to native apps downloaded from an app store.

- *Minimal use of data*: Data are fetched for users only when necessary.

The App Shell Model is great to use in apps with a service worker. We can cache our application shell so that it works offline and populates its content using JS.

Our App

In this book, we are going to build VueNoteApp (Figure 1-17). It is a simple notebook app that allows us to collect memos if our phone is also connected with Firebase and to update information when we are online.

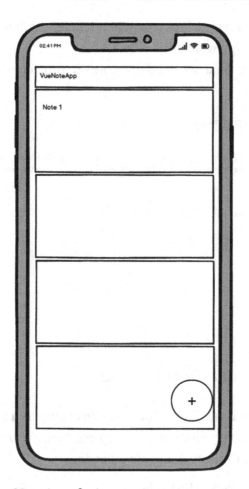

Figure 1-17. *VueNoteApp design*

In each chapter, we learn a new skill and extend the functionality of VueNoteApp. You can find all the source code at

```
https://github.com/carlosrojaso/appress-book-pwa
```

I suggest you clone this repo and use it to unblock when you don't get the expected results as you follow along step-by-step in each chapter. I separate the code by steps. You can go to a specific stage using

```
$git checkout [version]
```

I've included [version] for you. When I include it in this book, you can go there when you want.

Let's get started. First, we need to create our project using Vue CLI (Figure 1-18):

```
$vue create vue-note-app
```

```
Projects — node ~/.nvm/versions/node/v10.0.0/bin/vue create vue-note-app — 73×19
Carloss-MacBook-Pro:Projects carlosrojaso$ vue create vue-note-app


Vue CLI v3.10.0
? Please pick a preset: (Use arrow keys)
> default (babel, eslint)
  Manually select features
```

Figure 1-18. *Vue CLI create command*

We want a folder called vue-note-app that contains a bunch of files that reflect the basic structure in a Vue project. Next, we open this project from Visual Studio Code by doing the following:

1. Open Visual Studio Code.

2. Go to File ➤ Open... (Figure 1-19).

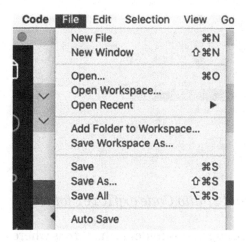

Figure 1-19. *Visual Studio Code Open folder*

3. Search for the vue-note-app folder in your
    computer and select it (Figure 1-20).

Figure 1-20. *vue-note-app folder*

You should see all the files from the project in your editor (Figure 1-21).

Figure 1-21. *Visual Studio Code* `explorer` *folder*

The important thing in this folder is that `src` is where we write our code (Figure 1-22).

Figure 1-22. *Visual Studio Code* `src` *file*

From the terminal, when Vue CLI finishes, run the following commands in your terminal:

```
$cd vue-note-app
```

```
$npm run serve
```

Now visit `http://localhost:8080`. You should see the page shown in Figure 1-23.

Figure 1-23. *Vue project* `npm run serve`

Congratulations! You have your first app in Vue.js. You can go there from the repo (`https://github.com/carlosrojaso/appress-book-pwa`) with

`$git checkout v1.0.1`

Now we can check out the appearance on mobile screens. To do this, we use Chrome DevTools. Right click the Chrome tab and select Inspect (as shown in Figure 1-24) or press Command+Option+C (Mac) or Control+Shift+C (Windows, Linux, Chrome OS).

Figure 1-24. *Google Chrome right click ➤ Inspect*

Select "Dock side" at the top right of the screen (Figure 1-25).

Figure 1-25. *Google Chrome DevTools change to dock side*

After that, you should see Chrome DevTools docked to the side (Figure 1-26).

Figure 1-26. *Google Chrome DevTools in side view*

Choose the toggle device toolbar (the top right icon in Figure 1-27) or press Command+Shift+M (Mac).

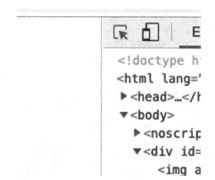

Figure 1-27. *Google Chrome DevTools toogle device toolbar*

And now we can see our app as a mobile app (Figure 1-28).

Figure 1-28. *Google Chrome iPhone 5/SE view*

You can switch the screen resolution by accessing the device drop-down menu (Figure 1-29).

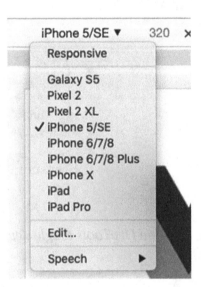

Figure 1-29. *Google Chrome DevTools device views*

I prefer to work with iPhone 5/SE screen resolution because it is a good point of reference with regard to aspect in the development environment. Now let's add Vuetify to our project:

```
$npm install vuetify --save
```

We need go to the file src/main.js and add

```
import Vue from 'vue'
import App from './App.vue'
import Vuetify from 'vuetify'

import 'vuetify/dist/vuetify.min.css'

Vue.config.productionTip = false
Vue.use(Vuetify)

new Vue({
  render: h => h(App),
}).$mount('#app')
```

Note   main.js is the main entry JS file that drives our app. If you see this file, you'll notice we are importing the Vue library and the App.vue component. Later, we create a Vue instance. A Vue instance is an object that represents our root component, which represents our application.

Now we can use Vuetify components, but we want to use icons too. To do this, we need to add the Material Icons fonts to the file public/index.html:

Note   Material Icons fonts are an easy way to add the appearance and the styling in Material Design guidelines.

```
<head>
...
        <link href='https://fonts.googleapis.com/css?family=
        Roboto:100,300,400,500,700,900|Material+Icons' rel=
        "stylesheet">
...
</head>
```

In addition, we need make some changes in the file src/App.vue in
<template></template>:

Note   App.vue is a file component in the Vue world. It contains three
chunks of code—HTML, CSS, and JS—which I mentioned earlier. It
can be tricky to understand at the beginning, but it is a great way to
create self-contained components that have all we need in a single file.

```
<template>
  <v-app>
    <v-toolbar app>
        <v-icon>arrow_back</v-icon>
      <v-toolbar-title >
        <span>VueNoteApp</span>
      </v-toolbar-title>
      <v-spacer></v-spacer>
    </v-toolbar>

    <v-content>
      <img alt="Vue logo" src="./assets/logo.png">
      <HelloWorld msg="Welcome to Your Vue.js App"/>
    </v-content>
  </v-app>
</template>
```

In the previous code, we added `<v-toolbar>` and `<v-content>` components, which are provided for Vuetify. In Vue.js, we build new blocks to show in our browser. These blocks are called *Vue components*, and we name them in a way that makes sense to us. One way to understand Vue components is to think of `<audio>` or `<video>` tags in HTML5. You know that when you add them to your HTML, an audio or video player is going to show up.

If everything is okay, you should be able to see our app with a Material Design user experience/UI (Figure 1-30).

Figure 1-30. *VueNoteApp with Material toolbar*

You can go there from `repo` (`https://github.com/carlosrojaso/ appress-book-pwa`) with

`$git checkout v1.0.2`

Building Our Manifest

The manifest file is a way to indicate to web browsers, and especially mobile devices, that our web app can be installed and how to display it. It is a JSON file in which we specify several properties along with their values.

The manifest is placed at the root of our application in a file called `manifest.json`. In it, we specify things such as the name of the application, the icon or icons of the application, a name, whether it should be shown vertically or horizontally, themes and colors that align with the look and feel of your site, and so on.

To generate the manifest, we use a generator for now. However, in Chapter 2, we create the manifest from scratch.

```
https://app-manifest.firebaseapp.com/
```

Our icon to upload is located here:

```
https://github.com/carlosrojaso/appress-book-pwa/blob/
c9191ea119ecd0d7ebe0053cde0cdc909b877780/public/icons/icon-
512x512.png
```

We place the following options and generate the icons. The generator creates the JSON we need and we attach it to our app (Figure 1-31).

Figure 1-31. *Web app manifest generator*

At the end, you should see something similar to the following:

```
{
"name": "VueNoteApp",
"short_name": "VueNoteApp",
"theme_color": "#36495d",
"background_color": "#36495d",
"display": "standalone",
"orientation": "portrait",
"Scope": "/",
"start_url": "/",
"icons": [
{
"src": "./icons/icon-72x72.png",
"sizes": "72x72",
"type": "image/png"
},
```

```json
{
"src": "./icons/icon-96x96.png",
"sizes": "96x96",
"type": "image/png"
},
{
"src": "./icons/icon-128x128.png",
"sizes": "128x128",
"type": "image/png"
},
{
"src": "./icons/icon-144x144.png",
"sizes": "144x144",
"type": "image/png"
},
{
"src": "./icons/icon-152x152.png",
"sizes": "152x152",
"type": "image/png"
},
{
"src": "./icons/icon-192x192.png",
"sizes": "192x192",
"type": "image/png"
},
{
"src": "./icons/icon-384x384.png",
"sizes": "384x384",
"type": "image/png"
},
```

```
{
"src": "./icons/icon-512x512.png",
"sizes": "512x512",
"type": "image/png"
}
],
"splash_pages": null
}
```

When you press the Generate ZIP button, you will have the icon along with the JSON file in a compressed file. Just move them to public/folder.

Next we need to tell our web app that a manifest file exists. To do this, add the following line to index.html:

```
<link rel="manifest" href="/manifest.json">
```

You can go there from the repo (https://github.com/carlosrojaso/appress-book-pwa) with

```
$git checkout v1.0.3
```

```
$npm run serve
```

Now to check manifest.json. We open Chrome DevTools and select the Application tab. From there, we select Manifest. By doing so, information about our app appears on the screen (Figure 1-32).

Figure 1-32. *Google Chrome DevTools manifest properties view*

At this point, we have two of the three requirements needed to convert our app to a PWA: a web manifest and an app icon. In the next section, we create the service worker.

Creating Our Service Worker

A service worker is a script (JS file) that runs in the background, regardless of whether a web page is open. It is necessary to add features such as offline support and push notifications, among others.

To create our service worker, we use a library called Workbox (for more information, go to `https://developers.google.com/web/tools/workbox/`), which is the successor of sw-toolbox and sw-precache (for more information, go to `https://github.com/GoogleChromeLabs/sw-toolbox` and `https://github.com/GoogleChromeLabs/sw-precache`). We installed this in the "Getting Started" section of this chapter.

You can check whether Workbox is working in your machine by running

```
$ workbox --version
```

The Workbox version should show up onscreen.

Now, from the project root, we generate a service worker with the command

```
$ workbox wizard
```

This starts a configuration wizard in our terminal. We answer the question asked so that it generates a file (Figure 1-33). We select public/.

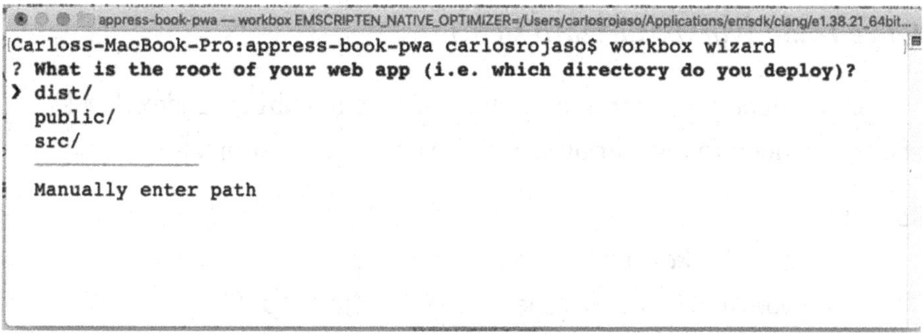

```
● ○ ●    appress-book-pwa — workbox EMSCRIPTEN_NATIVE_OPTIMIZER=/Users/carlosrojaso/Applications/emsdk/clang/e1.38.21_64bit...
Carloss-MacBook-Pro:appress-book-pwa carlosrojaso$ workbox wizard
? What is the root of your web app (i.e. which directory do you deploy)?
> dist/
  public/
  src/
  ─────────────────────────
  Manually enter path
```

Figure 1-33. *Workbox wizard step 1*

As shown in Figure 1-34, we select all options.

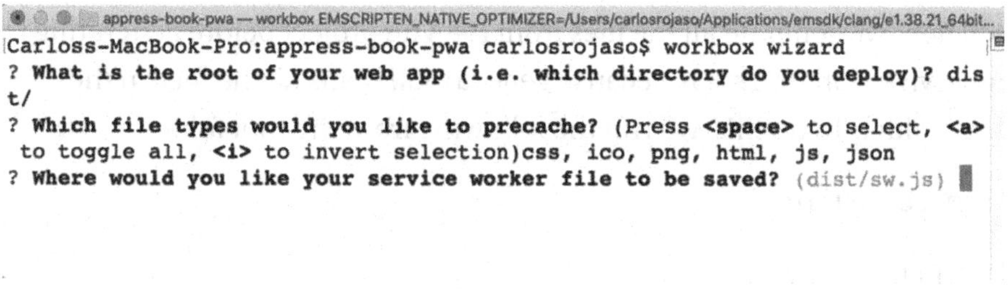

```
● ○ ●    appress-book-pwa — workbox EMSCRIPTEN_NATIVE_OPTIMIZER=/Users/carlosrojaso/Applications/emsdk/clang/e1.38.21_64bit...
Carloss-MacBook-Pro:appress-book-pwa carlosrojaso$ workbox wizard
? What is the root of your web app (i.e. which directory do you deploy)? dis
t/
? Which file types would you like to precache? (Press <space> to select, <a>
  to toggle all, <i> to invert selection)css, ico, png, html, js, json
? Where would you like your service worker file to be saved? (dist/sw.js)
```

Figure 1-34. *Workbox wizard step 2*

Figure 1-35 shows how we can select the default value (dist/sw.js) and press Enter. Later, we can select the other default value (workbox-config.js) and press Enter.

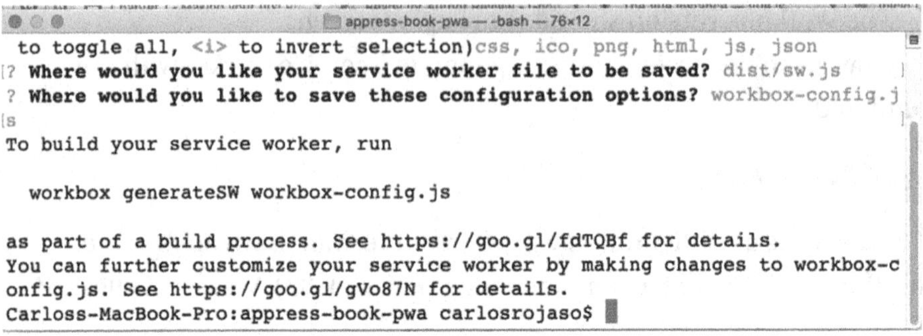

```
● ● ●                    appress-book-pwa — -bash — 76×12
 to toggle all, <i> to invert selection)css, ico, png, html, js, json
[? Where would you like your service worker file to be saved? dist/sw.js      ]
 ? Where would you like to save these configuration options? workbox-config.j
[s                                                                            ]
To build your service worker, run

  workbox generateSW workbox-config.js

as part of a build process. See https://goo.gl/fdTQBf for details.
You can further customize your service worker by making changes to workbox-c
onfig.js. See https://goo.gl/gVo87N for details.
Carloss-MacBook-Pro:appress-book-pwa carlosrojaso$ █
```

Figure 1-35. *Workbox wizard step 3*

Next we need to perform an additional step in public/index.html, because we need to register our service worker in our project:

```
<script>
    if ('serviceWorker' in navigator) {
      window.addEventListener('load', function() {
        navigator.serviceWorker.register('/sw.js');
      });
    }
</script>
```

Then, we generate all the files from the Vue project before generating the service worker. This is because generateSW scans all the files in the dist/ folder. To do this, we run the following from the root folder:

```
$ npm run build
```

And then we run

```
$ workbox generate:sw workbox-config.js
```

Now, if you open /dist/sw.js, you should see something like

```
/**
 * Welcome to your Workbox-powered service worker!
 *
 * You'll need to register this file in your web app and you
   should
 * disable HTTP caching for this file too.
 * See https://goo.gl/nhQhGp
 *
 * The rest of the code is auto-generated. Please don't update
   this file
 * directly; instead, make changes to your Workbox build
   configuration
 * and re-run your build process.
 * See https://goo.gl/2aRDsh
 */

importScripts("https://storage.googleapis.com/workbox-cdn/
releases/4.3.0/workbox-sw.js");

self.addEventListener('message', (event) => {
  if (event.data && event.data.type === 'SKIP_WAITING') {
    self.skipWaiting();
  }
});

/**
 * The workboxSW.precacheAndRoute() method efficiently caches
   and responds to
 * requests for URLs in the manifest.
 * See https://goo.gl/S9QRab
 */
self.__precacheManifest = [
```

```
{
  "url": "favicon.ico",
  "revision": "1ba2ae710d927f13d483fd5d1e548c9b"
},
{
  "url": "icons/icon-128x128.png",
  "revision": "ffaadd7090ccc9894c343dc6edcf7d63"
},
{
  "url": "icons/icon-144x144.png",
  "revision": "4eb27c4935821238c7bc0ca80a20b63d"
},
{
  "url": "icons/icon-152x152.png",
  "revision": "7b77bf7ba95c6157993e8f8d576cbe27"
},
{
  "url": "icons/icon-192x192.png",
  "revision": "32c1b8e4c143af7fd3ea577946dc133a"
},
{
  "url": "icons/icon-384x384.png",
  "revision": "13c5a5b2b57f768a89cfc71cce51e6bd"
},
{
  "url": "icons/icon-512x512.png",
  "revision": "577afa5f8be8a0be114f8f83e14bc73e"
},
```

```
  {
    "url": "icons/icon-72x72.png",
    "revision": "6f7bf21f0a3ddb87395d77d0f77432aa"
  },
  {
    "url": "icons/icon-96x96.png",
    "revision": "60c33f9b23cc43fe1d884a4dfe7b6032"
  },
  {
    "url": "index.html",
    "revision": "ddfe356a2e66115d4924f9e5a1294ba2"
  },
  {
    "url": "manifest.json",
    "revision": "2c956a55ebdeb23295c6ad907fc29b4f"
  }
].concat(self.__precacheManifest || []);
workbox.precaching.precacheAndRoute(self.__precacheManifest,
{});
```

Note   sw.js is different each time because when we run $npm
run build, Vue CLI generates new files from our Vue project. Then
we run $workbox generate:sw each time.

And now we have the last of the three requirements in our web app to
become a PWA: a service worker

Because $npm run serve is a development server and we need to test
our app in a production environment, we need to take some extra steps
here. The official Vue.js documents suggest installing the package serve
(https://github.com/zeit/serve). You can find more information at
https://cli.vuejs.org/guide/deployment.html#general-guidelines.
serve is a simple way to serve static files. To be ready, we need to run

```
$npm install -g serve
```

and then run

```
$serve -s dist
```

You should now see something like what is shown in Figure 1-36. Next, we test our first PWA!

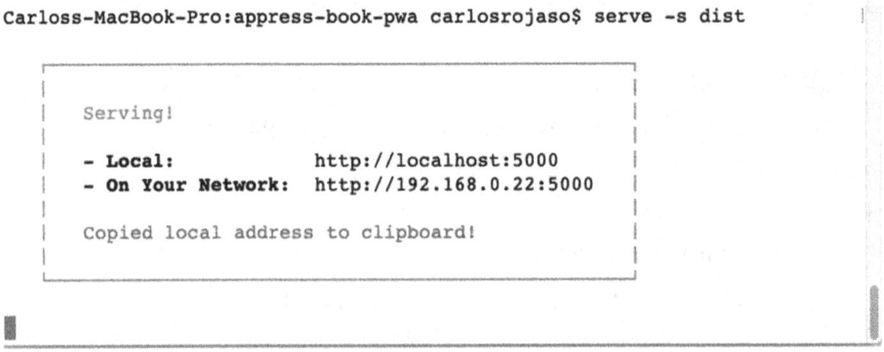

```
Carloss-MacBook-Pro:appress-book-pwa carlosrojaso$ serve -s dist

    Serving!

    - Local:           http://localhost:5000
    - On Your Network: http://192.168.0.22:5000

    Copied local address to clipboard!
```

Figure 1-36. *Running our PWA in a production environment*

We check the service worker in Chrome DevTools in the Application tab (Figure 1-37).

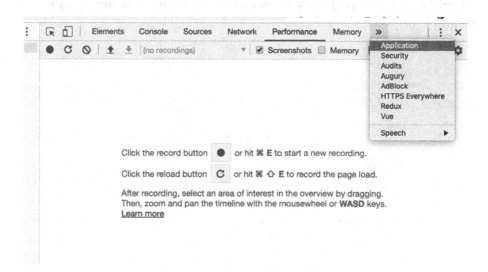

Figure 1-37. *Google Chrome DevTools Application tab*

It's a good practice to clear our storage each time we test our PWA, because we save data in our browser. If we skip this step, we may get unexpected results. To do this, we need only go to the Clear storage tab (Figure 1-38).

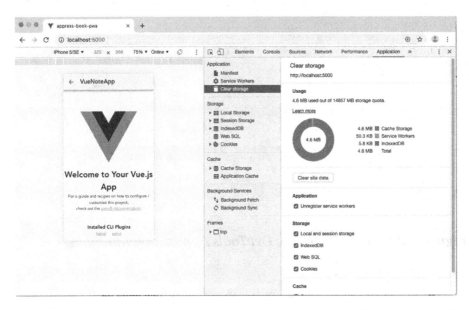

Figure 1-38. *Google Chrome DevTools Application* ➤ *Clear storage tab*

Now select Service Workers from the Application tab. You should see something like what is shown in Figure 1-39.

Figure 1-39. *Google Chrome DevTools Service Workers option*

We can test the offline feature by clicking the Offline check box and refreshing our app (Figure 1-40).

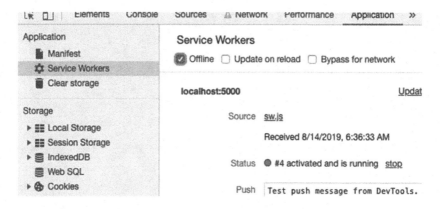

Figure 1-40. *Google Chrome DevTools Service Workers offline option*

This means our PWA is ready. Congratulations!

One last thing. Each time we make changes in our service worker or in our app we need to run

```
$ npm run build
$ workbox generate:sw workbox-config.js
$serve -s dist
```

You can go there from the repo with

```
$git checkout v1.0.4
```

Summary

PWAs are web applications that provide a native mobile app experience. You can install these apps on your devices, access them offline, and interact with them without having the app active. Push notifications are an example of this.

Progressive applications are a general web site. That is, they'll have the regular structure of a web app or SPA, with an index (index.html) and HTML, CSS, and JS files. In addition to this, to be considered a PWA, it must contain a manifest file, an app icon, and service workers.

CHAPTER 2

Web App Manifest

The `manifest` file is a way to tell web browsers, and especially mobile devices, how to show your app. It is basically a JSON file in which you specify many properties along with their values.

Creating Our Manifest

In Chapter 1, we created the `manifest` file with a generator. In this chapter, we create it from scratch to acquire an understanding of its properties.

To begin, we create a file in the root at the same level of the main entry (usually `index.html`) with the name `manifest.json` and add

```
{}
```

Our file is now ready, but we need to add some properties so that web and mobile browsers understand which properties to use when installing our app.

name

name provides a name for the site when displayed to the user.

```
"name": "VueNoteApp",
```

© Carlos Rojas 2020
C. Rojas, *Building Progressive Web Applications with Vue.js*,
https://doi.org/10.1007/978-1-4842-5334-2_2

short_name

short_name provides a short name for the application. This property is similar to name, but is used when there is insufficient space to display the full name of the PWA.

```
"short_name": "VueNoteApp",
```

theme_color

theme_color defines the default theme color for an application.

```
"theme_color": "#36495d",
```

background_color

background_color defines the expected background color for the web site.

```
"background_color": "#36495d",
```

description

description provides a general description of what the pinned web site does.

```
"description": "Our first Progressive Web App using VueJS",
```

display

display defines the developers' preferred display mode for the web site.

```
"display": "standalone",
```

You can use also `fullscreen`, `minimal-ui`, and `browser`. For more information, go to `https://developer.mozilla.org/en-US/docs/Web/Manifest#display`. With `standalone`, we can show our app as a regular native app with an icon.

orientation

`orientation` defines the default orientation for the web site's top-level browsing contexts.

```
"orientation": "portrait",
```

You can find more orientation values at `https://developer.mozilla.org/en-US/docs/Web/Manifest/orientation`. With `portrait`, we can show our app as apps are usually seen in mobile devices.

scope

`scope` restricts the web pages that can be viewed. If, while you are in your app, you navigate to an app that is out of scope, a regular browser window is opened. For example, if, in my app, I have `/app` and `/assets` from the root folder and I choose `"scope": "/app"` and try to call `/assets/logo.png`, this opens a new tab in the web browser because it is out of the context of my app.

```
"scope": "/app",
```

start_url

`start_url` specifies the main entry point (usually `index.html`) when you add to the home screen.

```
"start_url": "/",
```

icons

icons specifies an array of image files that can serve as application icons, depending on context.

```
"icons": [
{
        "src": "./icons/icon-72x72.png",
        "sizes": "72x72",
        "type": "image/png"
},
{
        "src": "./icons/icon-96x96.png",
        "sizes": "96x96",
        "type": "image/png"
},
{
        "src": "./icons/icon-128x128.png",
        "sizes": "128x128",
        "type": "image/png"
},
{
        "src": "./icons/icon-144x144.png",
        "sizes": "144x144",
        "type": "image/png"
},
{
        "src": "./icons/icon-152x152.png",
        "sizes": "152x152",
        "type": "image/png"
},
```

```
{
        "src": "./icons/icon-192x192.png",
        "sizes": "192x192",
        "type": "image/png"
},
{

        "src": "./icons/icon-384x384.png",
        "sizes": "384x384",
        "type": "image/png"
},
{

        "src": "./icons/icon-512x512.png",
        "sizes": "512x512",
        "type": "image/png"
}
],
```

The Final Manifest

Putting all the parts together, we have a manifest.json file with properties
and values for VueNoteApp.

```
{
        "name": "VueNoteApp",
        "short_name": "VueNoteApp",
        "theme_color": "#36495d",
        "background_color": "#36495d",
        "display": "standalone",
        "orientation": "portrait",
        "scope": "/",
        "start_url": "/",
```

```
"icons": [
{
        "src": "./icons/icon-72x72.png",
        "sizes": "72x72",
        "type": "image/png"
},
{
        "src": "./icons/icon-96x96.png",
        "sizes": "96x96",
        "type": "image/png"
},
{
        "src": "./icons/icon-128x128.png",
        "sizes": "128x128",
        "type": "image/png"
},
{
        "src": "./icons/icon-144x144.png",
        "sizes": "144x144",
        "type": "image/png"
},
{
        "src": "./icons/icon-152x152.png",
        "sizes": "152x152",
        "type": "image/png"
},
{
        "src": "./icons/icon-192x192.png",
        "sizes": "192x192",
        "type": "image/png"
},
```

```
        {
                "src": "./icons/icon-384x384.png",
                "sizes": "384x384",
                "type": "image/png"
        },
        {

                "src": "./icons/icon-512x512.png",
                "sizes": "512x512",
                "type": "image/png"

        }
        ]
}
```

Linking Our Manifest in Our App

Adding the manifest to our app is easy. We just link it in the main entry (usually index.html):

```
<link rel="manifest" href="/manifest.json">
```

You can go there from the repo (https://github.com/carlosrojaso/appress-book-pwa) with

```
$git checkout v1.0.5
```

Debugging Our Web App Manifest

To see if everything works fine, we need to open Chrome DevTools and locate the Application tab (Figure 2-1).

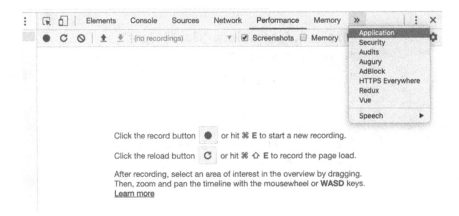

Figure 2-1. *Google Chrome DevTools Application tab*

From it, we select Manifest (Figure 2-2).

Figure 2-2. *Google Chrome DevTools manifest properties view. In this tab you can see how the web browser is understanding your properties in the web app manifest*

Summary

The web app manifest is a JSON file that tells web browsers, and especially mobile devices, how to show your app. It delineates the name, icons, and background color, among other things.

CHAPTER 3

Service Workers

There are common scenarios in which web applications are limited by not having an active window tab in the Web browser. However, if we take our app to the mobile world, this limitation does not exists, because even though a mobile app is closed, we can interact with the user by using, for example, push notifications. Service workers are the best option for adding special capabilities to web apps, which make them feel natural when they are installed from a mobile device (without users having to "enter" an app store or Google Play).

The Web is evolving. We can now create mechanisms that give users similar experiences in both apps and browsers, which led to the development of PWAs and service workers.

What Is a Service Worker?

A service worker can be thought of as a script (JS file) that executes in the background, regardless of whether a web site is open. There are some exciting things about service workers:

- Service workers cannot access the document object model (DOM) directly. Service workers communicate with the pages that they control through the `PostMessage` interface, which manipulates the DOM if needed.

© Carlos Rojas 2020
C. Rojas, *Building Progressive Web Applications with Vue.js*,
https://doi.org/10.1007/978-1-4842-5334-2_3

- With service workers, we can control how network requests are handled.

- Service workers store information through IndexedDB, which I mentioned earlier. IndexedDB is a transactional database system found in web browsers. What do I need to use a service worker?

Service workers are great, but there are two things we must provide to integrate their benefits in our app:

1. Web browser support. You can see the actual support here: `https://caniuse.com/#feat= serviceworkers`

2. HTTPS in the server (except in localhost)

Understanding the Life Cycle

Service workers have a life cycle independent from web apps (Figure 3-1). Understanding the service worker's life cycle allows us to offer an excellent experience to our users.

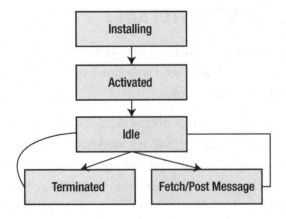

Figure 3-1. *The service worker life cycle*

Let's take a look at the states:

```
self.addEventListener('install', event => {
    // installing stage code
});
self.addEventListener('activate', event => {
    // activated stage code
});
self.addEventListener('fetch', event => {
    // fetch stage code
});
self.addEventListener('message', function(messageEvent) {
    // message stage code
})
```

- *Installing*: This is the first event that occurs. It is given just one time per service worker. If the called promise in this event fails, the web browser does discard it and won't let that the service worker take control of the client.

- *Activated*: After the service worker controls the client and is ready to handle events, the `activated` state is initiated. The service worker is now active.

- *Terminated and Fetch/Message*: After the service worker is in control of the pages, it can be in one of two states: `terminated` (to save memory) or `fetch/message` (to handle network requests).

57

Adding a Service Worker to an App

Now let's add a service worker to our app:

1. Create a JS file, sw.js, and locate it in the web
    project root (normally at the same level of the main
    entry). In Vue projects, we need to move this file to
    the public/ folder, because when we make a build,
    our tool takes this folder as our web app root.

2. Register the service worker by adding the following:

```
if ('serviceWorker' in navigator) {
  window.addEventListener('load', function() {
    navigator.serviceWorker.register('/sw.js').
    then(function(registration) {
      // Successful
      console.log('SW registered.');
    }, function(err) {
      // Error
      console.log('Something bad happened :(', err);
    });
  });
}
```

Core Technologies

Service workers allow adding new functionality thanks to some core
technologies. We look at them next.

Promises

Promises are an upgrade in the web platform to help in asynchronous scenarios. A promise is an object that represents a value in an asynchronous operation. A promise can take one of the following states:

- *pending*: Initial state

- *fulfilled*: The operation completed successfully

- *rejected*: The operation failed

We can create a basic promise using this syntax:

```
const myPromise = new Promise((resolve, reject) => {
        // fulfilled
        resolve(someValue);
        // rejected
        reject("failure reason");
});
```

And you can use this promise using then() and catch():

```
myPromise.then(
        (response) => {
        console.log("success!", response);
}
).catch(
        (error) => {
console.log("error!", error);
}
);
```

We use promises in each application programming interface (API) that we integrate into our script, which is why we must have a good understanding of this concept.

Fetch API

The fetch API is a new web interface that seeks to simplify XMLHttpRequest and provides more features that help the resource search through the network.

Its use looks like this:

```
var myImage = document.querySelector('img');

fetch('someimage.jpg').then(function(response) {
  return response.blob();
}).then(function(myBlob) {
  var objectURL = URL.createObjectURL(myBlob);
  myImage.src = objectURL;
});
```

As you can see, it works like a promise and allows for easy response management. In addition, thanks to its request and response objects, we have good control over the requests we intercept from the network.

Cache

Saving files locally is one of the most important advantages offered by PWAs. Let's think about that for a moment.

Mobile phone users often find themselves with very bad connections, such as when they are on a subway or when they are in a basement. Users just want to have a good experience with our services, which is why we need the cache API and the cache storage API to store important files locally, and respond with the app shell on all occasions. In this way, users don't have to wait for the PWA UI to load when they have an unstable connection.

Cache storage is the new storage layer; do not confuse it with the browser cache. To interact with cache storage we use the `cache` object:

```
caches.open(cacheName).then(function(cache) {
  // Cache code here
});
```

We find cache storage using Chrome DevTools in the Application tab and the Cache section (Figure 3-2).

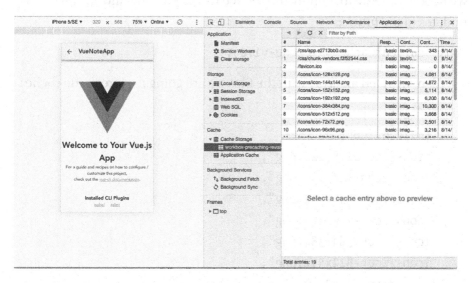

Figure 3-2. *Google Chrome DevTools cache storage section*

The previous code snippet shows the basic usage of `cache` storage API. The `cache` object allows us to carry out important operations. Here are a few:

- *`cache.addAll()`*: Adds an element array to cache storage.

- *`cache.delete()`*: Deletes an element from cache storage.

61

- *cache.match()*: Gets the first element that matches the sent parameter. If it is unable to find one, it sends an undefined.

- *cache.put()*: Allows for the addition of a new element to the cache.

Let's implement cache storage in our service worker. To do this, we create a version and some assets we want to store. In our new file sw.js, we need a variable to identify the service worker version and activate updates in the future:

```
const currentCache = 'cache-v1.0';
```

Also, we need an array with the files we are going to store in the cache:

```
const files = [
    "favicon.ico",
    "icons/icon-128x128.png",
    "icons/icon-144x144.png",
    "icons/icon-152x152.png",
    "icons/icon-192x192.png",
    "icons/icon-384x384.png",
    "icons/icon-512x512.png",
    "icons/icon-72x72.png",
    "icons/icon-96x96.png",
    "index.html",
    "manifest.json",
  ];
```

Moreover, we have to listen for install and activate events in the service worker life cycle. We then add our files to cache storage when we detect install, and update our files when currentCache has another version from an activate event:

```
self.addEventListener('install', event => {
  event.waitUntil(
    caches.open(currentCache).then(cache => {
      return cache.addAll(files);
    })
  );
});

self.addEventListener('activate', event => {
  event.waitUntil(
    caches.keys().then(cacheNames => Promise.all(
      cacheNames.filter(cacheName => {
        return cacheName !== currentCache
      }).map(cacheName => caches.delete(cacheName))
    ))
  );
});
```

You can go there from the repo (https://github.com/carlosrojaso/
appress-book-pwa) with

```
$git checkout v1.0.6
```

Debugging Our Service Worker

To see if everything works fine, we need to run

```
$npm run build
```

And then run

```
$serve -s dist
```

Next, open Chrome DevTools and locate the Application tab. Select
Service Workers. You should see information about your service worker
onscreen (Figure 3-3).

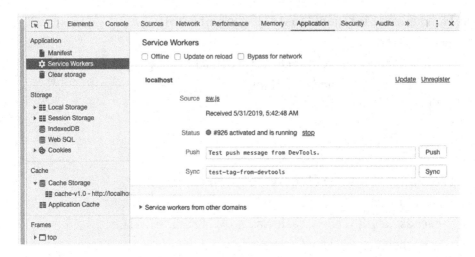

Figure 3-3. *Google Chrome DevTools service worker status activated and running*

At this point, we are saving some files in cache storage (Figure 3-4), but we don't have offline support because we are getting the files from the network. In Chapter 4, we learn how to get files from cache storage if we are offline.

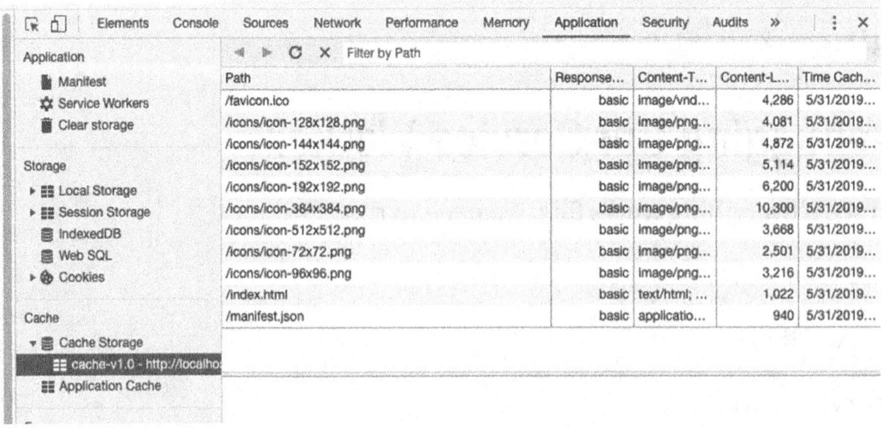

Figure 3-4. *Google Chrome DevTools cache storage section*

Summary

A service worker is a JS file that executes in the background, regardless of whether a web site is open. Thanks to service workers we can add support to a new world of Web APIS like CacheStorage and can use offline features to improve the user interaction with our Apps.

CHAPTER 4

Caching Strategies

Nowadays, most web apps run without offline capabilities. They depend almost totally on a server. We can observe this when, from our browser in a web app, we get disconnected and the dinosaur game appears onscreen. This is how Google Chrome tells us we are offline (Figure 4-1).

Figure 4-1. *Chrome dino game*

This is not the only scenario we want to avoid. There is also a common scenario in which LiFi shows neither our app nor the dinosaur, but leaves users waiting with a white browser window.

Some solutions work well to handle this nonconnection status, such as PouchDB or Firebase. However, with the use of web technologies such as service workers, IndexedDB, and the cache API, we can plan our offline strategies for our PWAs.

© Carlos Rojas 2020
C. Rojas, *Building Progressive Web Applications with Vue.js*,
https://doi.org/10.1007/978-1-4842-5334-2_4

When to Store Information

If you remember, a service worker has stages in its life cycle (Figure 4-2), beginning with when it is installed until it is terminated in a web app. These moments are perfect to start mechanisms that save, update, return, or delete data from cache storage. Let's look at some well-known strategies that can be applied to our PWAs.

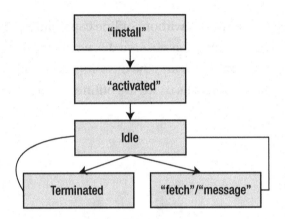

Figure 4-2. *The service worker life cycle*

The install event is the best moment to store files for the first time. If you remember the service worker life cycle, this stage is reached after it is detected in a web app. To reach it, we do something like this:

sw.js

```
const currentCache = 'cache-v1.0.0';

const files = [
    "favicon.ico",
    "icons/icon-128x128.png",
    "icons/icon-144x144.png",
    "icons/icon-152x152.png",
    "icons/icon-192x192.png",
```

```
    "icons/icon-384x384.png",
    "icons/icon-512x512.png",
    "icons/icon-72x72.png",
    "icons/icon-96x96.png",
    "index.html",
    "manifest.json",
];

self.addEventListener('install', event => {
  event.waitUntil(
    caches.open(currentCache).then(cache => {
      return cache.addAll(files);
    })
  );
});
```

You can go there from the repo (https://github.com/carlosrojaso/appress-book-pwa) with

```
$git checkout v1.0.7
```

As you can see, we have our files to store in the files array in our app shell. Next, we go in the install event, which brings the app shell elements from the network and stores them in cache storage, which then gives way to the activate event of the service worker (Figure 4-3).

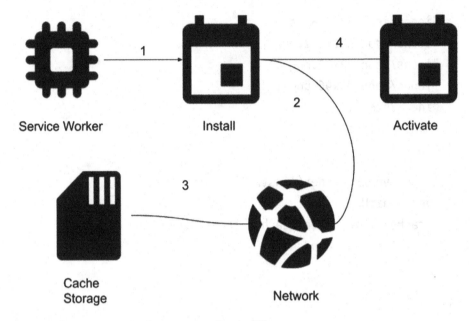

Figure 4-3. Saving data in an install *event*

When to Update Files in the Cache

Although it is supposed that the files in our app shell do not change frequently, they could do so, for example, with a user experience improvement, a branding change, and so on. We have to prepare for this moment and avoid saddling our users with version 1 of our app forever.

To handle a cache storage update, we use a version number in the name of our cache or the activated event of the service worker life cycle to eliminate older files and replace them with the new ones. Updating our service worker, looks something like this:

sw.js

```
const currentCache = 'cache-v1.0.0';

const files = [
    "favicon.ico",
    "icons/icon-128x128.png",
```

```
    "icons/icon-144x144.png",
    "icons/icon-152x152.png",
    "icons/icon-192x192.png",
    "icons/icon-384x384.png",
    "icons/icon-512x512.png",
    "icons/icon-72x72.png",
    "icons/icon-96x96.png",
    "index.html",
    "manifest.json",
];

self.addEventListener('install', event => {
  event.waitUntil(
    caches.open(currentCache).then(cache => {
      return cache.addAll(files);
    })
  );
});

self.addEventListener('activate', event => {
  let version = 'v1.0.0';
  event.waitUntil(
    caches.keys()
      .then(
        cacheNames => {
          Promise.all(
            cacheNames
              .map(c => c.split('-'))
              .filter(c => c[0] === 'cache')
              .filter(c => c[1] !== version)
              .map(c => caches.delete(c.join('-')))
          )
```

```
      }
    )
  );
});
```

You can go there from the repo (https://github.com/carlosrojaso/appress-book-pwa) with

```
$git checkout v1.0.8
```

If you look at the previous code, you'll see that we added a series of operations when our service worker gets to our `activate` event. We verify whether the name that it brings in `cacheNames` has the same version number that we have in `version`. If it doesn't, we delete the other cache that is detected (Figure 4-4). This ensures that previous versions, such as `cache-v0.0.0` or `cache-v0.0.1`, get deleted from the client's cache storage.

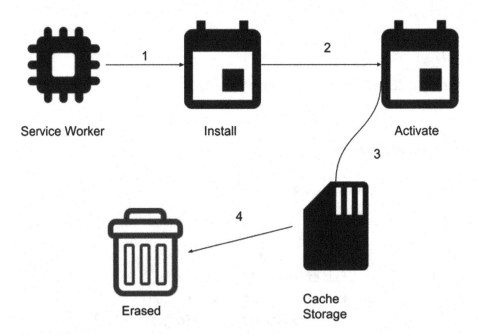

Figure 4-4. *Update data in* `activate` *event*

These two moments—when we store files in the cache and when we update cache storage—are usually common in every app.

Responding to Requests

Although there are many strategy mixes to respond to user requests, there are some identified patterns that work great with most apps.

The service worker triggers a `fetch` event when we make a request. It contains information about the fetch, including the request and how the receiver will treat the response:

sw.js

```
self.addEventListener("fetch", (event) => {
});
```

cacheFirst

The `cacheFirst` pattern responds to requests with files from cache storage. If the response from cache storage fails, it tries to respond with files from the network (Figure 4-5).

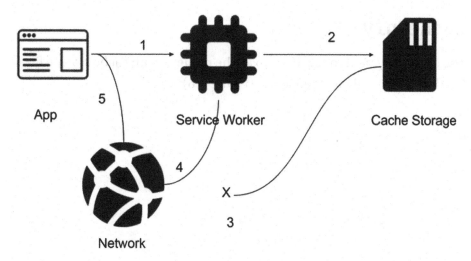

Figure 4-5. *cacheFirst strategy flow*

73

sw.js

```
self.addEventListener('fetch', event => {
    event.respondWith(
      caches.match(event.request).then(function(response) {
        return response || fetch(event.request);
      })
    );
});
```

> *Use case*: When your content changes infrequently,
> such as a corporate site. The content is always
> the same. You can save the files in the first use,
> provide a fast charge in the next uses, and update
> unfrequented changes in the content if this
> happens.

You can go there from the repo (`https://github.com/carlosrojaso/`
`appress-book-pwa`) with

```
$git checkout v1.0.9
```

cacheOnly

The cacheOnly pattern responds to all the requests with cache storage files.
If it does not find them, then it fails (Figure 4-6).

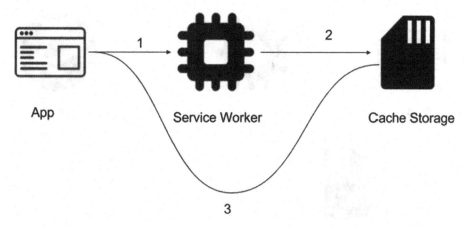

Figure 4-6. *cacheOnly strategy flow*

Its implementation is like this:

sw.js

```
self.addEventListener('fetch', event => {
  event.respondWith(caches.match(event.request));
});
```

> *Use case*: When you only want to access static files,
> such as a book that you can read offline. The content
> is fundamentally the same all the time.

You can go there from the repo (https://github.com/carlosrojaso/appress-book-pwa) with

```
$git checkout v1.0.10
```

networkFirst

The networkFirst pattern responds to all requests with network content. If it fails, it tries to respond with content from cache storage (Figure 4-7).

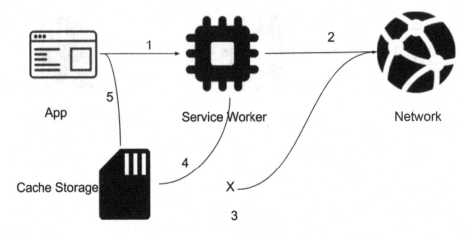

Figure 4-7. *networkFirst strategy flow*

Its implementation should look like this:

sw.js

```
self.addEventListener('fetch', event => {
    event.respondWith(
      fetch(event.request).catch(function() {
        return caches.match(event.request);
      })
    );
  });
```

> *Use case*: When your content is updated frequently,
> such as a blog that can be read offline. The content
> changes all the time and users want to read the
> latest content. However, if the user is offline, you can
> at least show the last stored content.

You can go there from the repo (https://github.com/carlosrojaso/
appress-book-pwa) with

```
$git checkout v1.0.11
```

stale-while-revalidate

The stale-while-revalidate pattern responds to all requests with cache content, if available, from cache storage; but, it also fetches an update from the network for next time (Figure 4-8).

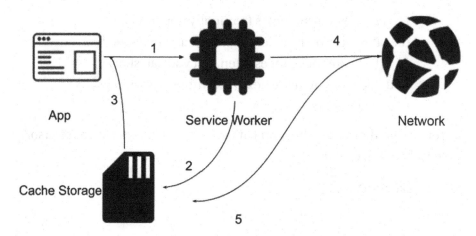

Figure 4-8. *stale-while-revalidate strategy flow*

sw.js

```
self.addEventListener('fetch', (event) => {
  event.respondWith(
    caches.open(currentCache)
    .then(function(cache) {
      return cache.match(event.request)
      .then(function(response) {
        var fetchPromise = fetch(event.request)
        .then(function(networkResponse) {
          cache.put(event.request, networkResponse.clone());
          return networkResponse;
        })
```

```
        return response || fetchPromise;
      })
    })
  );
});
```

> *Use case*: When content is frequently updated but
> the latest version is not critical, such as a news feed
> app. The content changes often, but you can show
> updated content in the next visit without providing a
> lousy experience for users.

You can go there from the repo (`https://github.com/carlosrojaso/`
`appress-book-pwa`) with

`$git checkout v1.0.12`

Updating Our App

At this point, we've looked at the manifest, service workers, and cache
strategies. Now, we can simplify our life with a package that we can install
using Vue CLI:

`$vue add @vue/pwa`

With this package, we add Workbox along with the official plug-in.
When you run the command, you'll see something like what is shown in
Figure 4-9.

```
●●●                             appress-book-pwa --- -bash --- 138×38
$ vue add @vue/pwa

🎁  Installing @vue/cli-plugin-pwa...

+ @vue/cli-plugin-pwa@3.8.0
updated 1 package in 16.631s
✔  Successfully installed plugin: @vue/cli-plugin-pwa

🚀  Invoking generator for @vue/cli-plugin-pwa...
✔  Successfully invoked generator for plugin: @vue/cli-plugin-pwa
   The following files have been updated / added:

     public/img/icons/android-chrome-192x192.png
     public/img/icons/android-chrome-512x512.png
     public/img/icons/apple-touch-icon-120x120.png
     public/img/icons/apple-touch-icon-152x152.png
     public/img/icons/apple-touch-icon-180x180.png
     public/img/icons/apple-touch-icon-60x60.png
     public/img/icons/apple-touch-icon-76x76.png
     public/img/icons/apple-touch-icon.png
     public/img/icons/favicon-16x16.png
     public/img/icons/favicon-32x32.png
     public/img/icons/msapplication-icon-144x144.png
     public/img/icons/mstile-150x150.png
     public/img/icons/safari-pinned-tab.svg
     public/robots.txt
     src/registerServiceWorker.js
     package-lock.json
     package.json
     public/manifest.json
     public/sw.js
     src/main.js
     workbox-config.js

   You should review these changes with git diff and commit them.

$ ▋
```

Figure 4-9. *Installing @vue/cli-plugin-pwa*

And the important thing is that, now when we run

$npm run build

we'll see the new service worker in our dist/ folder. Because of the previous changes, we need to keep our changes in the icons and manifest files.

Now we run our app:

$serve -s build

Figure 4-10 shows the console.

Figure 4-10. *Using @vue/cli-plugin-pwa in VueNoteApp*

If we take a look in cache storage, our files are there (Figure 4-11).

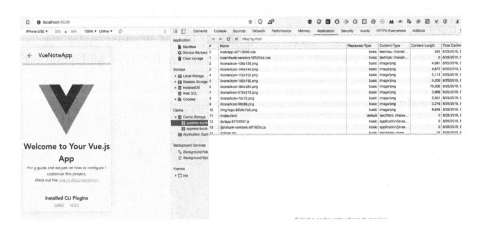

Figure 4-11. *Cache storage using @vue/cli-plugin-pwa in VueNoteApp*

You can go there from the repo (`https://github.com/carlosrojaso/appress-book-pwa`) with

```
$git checkout v1.0.13
```

Summary

With service workers, we can save assets and add offline support in our web apps. We looked at some patterns and good practices that help us deliver a better experience to our users. We also studied the events of the service worker life cycle to determine when to use storage capabilities effectively and efficiently.

CHAPTER 5

Working with Vue.js

Vue.js is an open source, progressive JS framework for building UIs that aim to be incrementally adoptable. The core library of Vue.js is focused on the view layer only, and is easy to pick up and integrate with other libraries or existing projects.

We'll see how to take advantage of its features to build fast, high-performance PWAs that work offline. We'll also build our notes app and examine key concepts for understanding the components of Vue.js.

What Are the Major Features of Vue.js?

Vue.js has all the features that a framework to build SPAs should have, but some stand out from all the others:

- *Virtual DOM*: Virtual DOM is a lightweight in-memory tree representation of the original HTML DOM and is updated without affecting the original DOM.

- *Components*: Components are used to create reusable custom elements in Vue.js applications.

- *Templates*: Vue.js provides HTML-based templates that bind the DOM with the Vue instance data.

© Carlos Rojas 2020
C. Rojas, *Building Progressive Web Applications with Vue.js*,
https://doi.org/10.1007/978-1-4842-5334-2_5

- *Routing*: Navigation between pages is achieved through vue-router.

- *Lightweight*: Vue.js is a lightweight library compared to other frameworks.

What Are Components?

Components are reusable elements for which we define their names and behavior. For an overview of the concept of components, look at Figure 5-1.

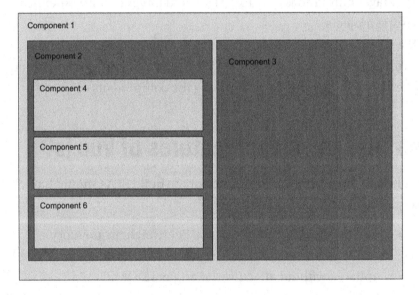

Figure 5-1. *Components in a web application*

You can see in Figure 5-1 that we have six components at different levels. Component 1 is the parent of components 2 and 3, and the grandparent of components 4, 5, and 6. We can make a hierarchical tree with this relationship (Figure 5-2).

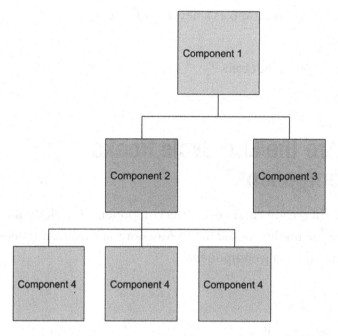

Figure 5-2. *Hierarchy of components*

Each component can be whatever we want it to be: a list, an image, a button, text, or whatever we define.

The fundamental way to define a simple component is

```
Vue.component('my-button', {
  data: function () {
    return {
      counter: 0
    }
  },
  template: '<button v-on:click="counter++">
  Clicks {{ counter }}.</button>'
})
```

We can add it to our app as a new HTML tag:

```
<div id="app">
  <my-button></my-button>
</div>
```

What Are the Life Cycle Hooks in a Component?

The process of creating and destroying components is called a life cycle. There are some methods used to run functions at specific moments. Consider the following component:

```
<script>
export default {
  name: 'HelloWorld',
  created: function () {
    console.log('Component created.');
  },
  mounted: function() {
    fetch('https://randomuser.me/api/?results=1')
    .then(
      (response) => {
        return response.json();
      }
    )
    .then(
      (reponseObject) => {
        this.email = reponseObject.results[0].email;
      }
    );
```

```
    console.log('Component is mounted.');
  },
  props: {
    msg: String,
    email:String
  }
}
</script>
```

Here, we added an e-mail property; we used `created()` and `mounted()`. These methods are called *life cycle hooks*, and we use them to do actions at specific moments in our component. For example, we make a call to an API when our component is mounted and get the e-mail at that moment.

You can go there from the repo (`https://github.com/carlosrojaso/appress-book-pwa`) with

`$git checkout lifecycles-chapter`

Life cycle hooks are an essential part of any serious component (Figure 5-3).

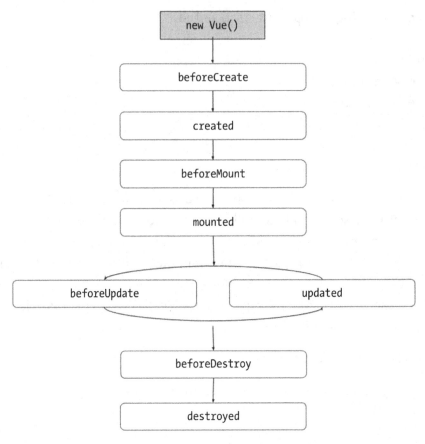

Figure 5-3. *Component life cycle hooks*

beforeCreate

The beforeCreate hook runs at the initialization of a component.

```
new Vue({
  beforeCreate: function () {
    console.log('Initialization is happening');
})
```

created

The created hook runs the component when it is initialized. You can then access reactive data, and events are active.

```
new Vue({
  created: function () {
    console.log('The Component is created');
})
```

beforeMount

The beforeMount hook runs right before the initial render happens and after the template or render functions have been compiled.

```
new Vue({
  beforeMount: function () {
    console.log('The component is going to be Mounted');
  }
})
```

mounted

With the mounted hook, you have full access to the reactive component, templates, and rendered DOM.

```
new Vue({
  mounted: function () {
    console.log('The component is mounted');
  }
})
```

beforeUpdate

The beforeUpdate hook runs after data changes in the component and the update cycle begins, right before the DOM is patched and rerendered.

```
new Vue({
  beforeUpdate: function () {
    console.log('The component is going to be updated');
  }
})
```

updated

The updated hook runs after data changes in the component and the DOM rerenders.

```
new Vue({
  updated: function () {
    console.log('The component is updated');
  }
})
```

beforeDestroy

The beforeDestroy hooks happens right before the component is destroyed. Your component is still fully present and functional.

```
new Vue({
  beforeDestroy: function () {
    console.log('The component is going to be destroyed');
  }
})
```

destroyed

The destroyed hook happens when everything attached to it has been destroyed. You might use the destroyed hook to do any last-minute cleanup.

```
new Vue({
  destroyed: function () {
    console.log('The component is destroyed');
  }
})
```

Communicating between Components

Components usually need to share information between them. For basic scenarios (Figure 5-4), we can use the props or ref attributes if we want to pass data to child components, emitters if we want to pass data to a parent component, and two-way data binding to have data sync between child and parents.

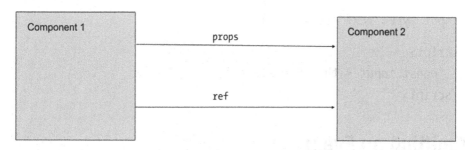

Figure 5-4. *A parent component communicating with a child component*

What Are Props?

Props are custom attributes you can register on a component. When a value is passed to a `prop` attribute, it becomes a property on that component instance. The basic structure is as follows:

```
Vue.component('some-item', {
  props: ['somevalue'],
  template: '<div>{{ somevalue }}</div>'
})
```

Now you can pass values like this:

```
<some-item somevalue="value for prop"></some-item>
```

What Is a `ref` attribute?

`ref` is used to register a reference to an element or a child component. The reference is registered under the parent component's `$refs` object. For more information, go to `https://vuejs.org/v2/api/#ref`. The basic structure is

```
<input type="text" ref="email">

<script>
    const input = this.$refs.email;
</script>
```

Emitting an Event

If you want a child to communicate with a parent, use `$emit()`, which is the recommended method to pass information or a call (Figure 5-5). A prop function is another way to pass information, but it's considered a bad practice and I do not discuss it.

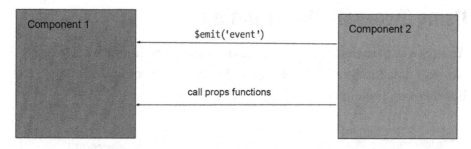

Figure 5-5. *A child component communicating with a parent component*

In Vue, we have the method $emit(), which we use to send data to parent components. The basic structure for emitting an event is

```
Vue.component('child-custom-component', {
  data: function () {
    return {
      customValue: 0
    }
  },
  methods: {
    giveValue: function () {
      this.$emit('give-value', this.customValue++)
    }
  },
  template: `
    <button v-on:click="giveValue">
      Click me for value
    </button>
  `
})
```

Using Two-way Data Binding

An easy way to maintain communication between components is to use two-way data binding. In this scenario, Vue.js makes communication between components for us (Figure 5-6).

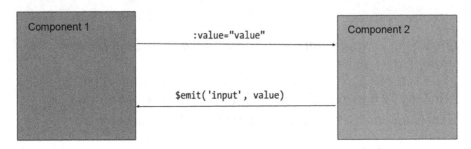

Figure 5-6. *Components communicating both ways*

Two-way data binding means that Vue.js syncs data properties and the DOM for you. Changes to a data property update the DOM, and changes made to the DOM update the data property; data move both ways. The basic structure to use two-way data binding is

```
new Vue({
    el: '#app',
    data: {
    somevalue: 'I am a two-way data value.'
    }
});
<input type="text" v-model="somevalue" value="A value">
```

What Is Vue Router?

Vue Router is an official routing plug-in for SPAs designed for use with the Vue.js framework. A router is a way to jump from one view to another in an SPA. Some of its features include the following:

- Nested route/view mapping

- Modular, component-based router configuration

- Route parameters, query, wildcards

- Fine-grained navigation control

- HTML5 history mode or hash mode, with autofallback in IE9

It is easy to integrate Vue Router in our Vue application.

1. Install the plug-in.

    ```
    $npm install vue-router
    ```

2. Add VueRouter in main.js.

    ```
    ...
    import VueRouter from 'vue-router'
    ...
    Vue.use(VueRouter);
    ```

3. Create routes in a new routes.js file.

    ```
    import HelloWorld from './components/HelloWorld.vue'

    export const routes = [
      {path: ", component: HelloWorld}
    ];
    ```

4. Create a VueRouter instance.

    ```
    const router = new VueRouter({routes});
    ```

5. Add VueRouter to Vue instance.

    ```
    const app = new Vue({
      router
    }).$mount('#app')
    ```

Building VueNoteApp

In Chapter 1, we started to develop VueNoteApp (Figure 5-7). In this section, we add the features we need in a basic note app using Vue.js.

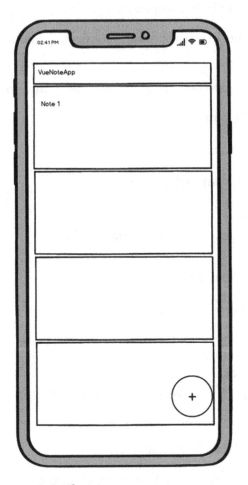

Figure 5-7. *VueNoteApp design*

Creating Notes

First of all, we need to create a button that allows us to add new notes and a view that shows us general information. We also need to show these notes in the main view. To do this, we need two extra components: Notes. vue and About.vue. The structure we need to create is

App.vue

```
components/Notes.vue
components/About.vue
```

Next we need to modify Apps.vue and tell it we need to use the Notes component here.

App.vue

```
<template>
  <v-app>
    <v-toolbar app>
        <v-icon>arrow_back</v-icon>
      <v-toolbar-title >
        <span>VueNoteApp</span>
      </v-toolbar-title>
      <v-spacer></v-spacer>
    </v-toolbar>

    <v-content>
      <img alt="Vue logo" src="./assets/logo.png">
      <Notes msg="Notes"/>
    </v-content>
  </v-app>
</template>
```

```
<script>
import Notes from './components/Notes.vue'

export default {
  name: 'app',
  components: {
    Notes
  }
}
</script>

<style>
#app {
  font-family: 'Avenir', Helvetica, Arial, sans-serif;
  -webkit-font-smoothing: antialiased;
  -moz-osx-font-smoothing: grayscale;
  text-align: center;
  color: #2c3e50;
  margin-top: 60px;
}
</style>
```

Then we must create a new components/Notes.vue file and write the necessary things for a component as you can see in the following code.

Notes.vue

```
<template>
  <div class="hello">
    <h1>{{ msg }}</h1>
  </div>
</template>
```

```
<script>
export default {
  name: 'Notes',
  props: {
    msg: String
  }
}
</script>

<!-- Add "scoped" attribute to limit CSS to this component only
-->
<style scoped>
h3 {
  margin: 40px 0 0;
}
ul {
  list-style-type: none;
  padding: 0;
}
li {
  display: inline-block;
  margin: 0 10px;
}
a {
  color: #42b983;
}
</style>
```

Now we are going to use an array (called pages) and save the notes there. In addition, We going to use v-for in our template to iterate in this array and add the elements in the DOM. In the Notes component, we need to emit an Add button to allow users to add a new note.

Notes.vue

```
<template>
  <div class="notes">
  <ul>
    <li v-for="(page, index) of pages" class="page">
      <div>{{page.title}} tit</div>
      <div>{{page.content}} cont</div>
     </li>
    <li class="new-note">
      <v-btn fab dark color="indigo" @click="newNote()">
        <v-icon dark>add</v-icon>
      </v-btn>
    </li>
  </ul>
  </div>
</template>

<script>
export default {
  name: 'Notes',
  props: ['pages'],
  methods: {
    newNote () {
    this.$emit('new-note')
    }
  }
}
</script>
```

```
<!-- Add "scoped" attribute to limit CSS to this component only
-->
<style scoped>
h3 {
  margin: 40px 0 0;
}
ul {
  list-style-type: none;
  padding: 0;
}
li {
  display: inline-block;
  margin: 0 10px;
}
a {
  color: #42b983;
}
</style>
```

Now we need to modify the App.vue component to send the pages array to the Notes component. Then we create a newNote function to add a new element to this array.

App.vue

```
<template>
  <v-app>
    <v-toolbar app>
      <v-toolbar-title >
        <span>VueNoteApp</span>
      </v-toolbar-title>
      <v-spacer></v-spacer>
```

```
    <v-toolbar-items>
      <v-btn flat>About</v-btn>
    </v-toolbar-items>
  </v-toolbar>

  <v-content>
    <Notes :pages="pages" @new-note="newNote"/>
  </v-content>
</v-app>
</template>

<script>
import Notes from './components/Notes.vue'

export default {
  name: 'app',
  components: {
    Notes
  },
  data: () => ({
    pages:[],
    index:0
  }),
  methods:  {
    newNote () {
      this.pages.push({
        title: ",
        content: "
      });
      console.log(this.pages);
    },
    saveNote () {

    },
```

```
    deleteNote () {

    }
  }
}
</script>

<style>
#app {
  font-family: 'Avenir', Helvetica, Arial, sans-serif;
  -webkit-font-smoothing: antialiased;
  -moz-osx-font-smoothing: grayscale;
  text-align: center;
  color: #2c3e50;
  margin-top: 60px;
}
</style>
```

At this point, use $npm run serve and make sure you see something like what is shown in Figure 5-8.

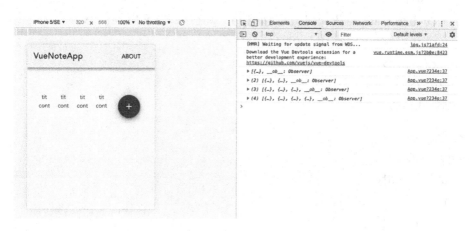

Figure 5-8. *VueNoteApp creating notes*

You can go there from the repo (`https://github.com/carlosrojaso/appress-book-pwa`) with

```
$git checkout v1.1.0
```

Next we are going to polish the styles in our app using Vuetify components and CSS.

Notes.vue

```
<template>
  <div class="notes">
    <v-card v-for="(page, index) in pages" :key="index">
      <v-card-title primary-title>
        <div>
          <h3 class="headline mb-0">{{page.title}} tit +
          {{index}}</h3>
          <div> {{page.content}} tit </div>
        </div>
      </v-card-title>
    </v-card>
    <v-btn fab dark color="indigo" @click="newNote()">
      <v-icon dark>add</v-icon>
    </v-btn>
  </div>
</template>

<script>
export default {
  name: 'Notes',
  props: ['pages'],
  methods: {
    newNote () {
    this.$emit('new-note')
    }
```

```
  }
}
</script>

<!-- Add "scoped" attribute to limit CSS to this component only
-->
<style scoped>
a {
  color: #42b983;
}
</style>
```

App.vue

```
<template>
  <v-app>
    <v-toolbar app>
      <v-toolbar-title >
        <span>VueNoteApp</span>
      </v-toolbar-title>
      <v-spacer></v-spacer>
      <v-toolbar-items>
        <v-btn flat>About</v-btn>
      </v-toolbar-items>
    </v-toolbar>

    <v-content>
      <Notes :pages="pages" @new-note="newNote"/>
    </v-content>
  </v-app>
</template>
```

```
<script>
import Notes from './components/Notes.vue'

export default {
  name: 'app',
  components: {
    Notes
  },
  data: () => ({
    pages:[],
    index:0
  }),
  methods:  {
    newNote () {
      this.pages.push({
        title: 'Title',
        content: 'Lorem ipsum dolor sit amet, consectetur
        adipiscing elit. Vivamus et elit id purus accumsan
        lacinia. Suspendisse nulla urna, facilisis ac tincidunt
        in, accumsan sit amet enim. Donec a ante dolor'
      });
    },
    saveNote () {

    },
    deleteNote () {

    }
  }
}
</script>
```

```
<style>
#app {
  font-family: 'Avenir', Helvetica, Arial, sans-serif;
  -webkit-font-smoothing: antialiased;
  -moz-osx-font-smoothing: grayscale;
  text-align: center;
  color: #2c3e50;
  margin-top: 60px;
}
</style>
```

With these small changes, you should now see something like what is shown in Figure 5-9.

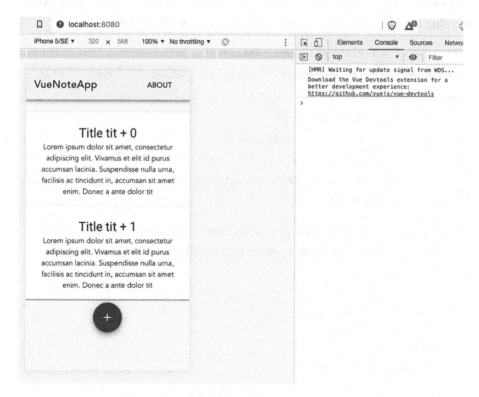

Figure 5-9. *Polishing styling*

You can go there from the repo (`https://github.com/carlosrojaso/appress-book-pwa`) with

```
$git checkout v1.1.1
```

Adding a Form

Thus far we've provided the capability of adding notes by pushing a button, but now we need to allow users to enter their notes. To do this, we need to add a form. And to keep our app simple, we are going to use v-dialog—which is a component that shows us a beautiful modal window where we can put the form—in the App.vue component. In addition, we need to sync the data in the form with the component. To do this, we need to create two variables—newTitle and newContent—and use two-way data binding in App.vue using the directive v-model with the form:

```
<v-flex xs12 sm12 md12>
<v-text-field v-model="newTitle" value="" label="Title*"
required></v-text-field>
    </v-flex>
    <v-flex xs12 sm12 md12>
      <v-textarea v-model="newContent" value=""
      label="Content"></v-textarea>
    </v-flex>
```

As you can see, we added v-model="newTitle" and v-model= "newContent", and created two properties with the same name in the component data.

```
data: () => ({
  ...
  newTitle: ",
  newContent: ",
  ...
}),
```

By adding v-model, Vue.js takes care of updating the data and the template for us. Together, all the code looks like this:

App.vue

```
<template>
  <v-app>
    <v-toolbar app>
      <v-toolbar-title >
        <span>VueNoteApp</span>
      </v-toolbar-title>
      <v-spacer></v-spacer>
      <v-toolbar-items>
        <v-btn flat>About</v-btn>
      </v-toolbar-items>
    </v-toolbar>

    <v-content>
      <Notes :pages="pages" @new-note="newNote"/>
    </v-content>
    <v-dialog v-model="dialog">
    <v-card>
      <v-card-title>
        <span class="headline">New Note</span>
      </v-card-title>
      <v-card-text>
        <v-container grid-list-md>
          <v-layout wrap>
            <v-flex xs12 sm12 md12>
                <v-text-field v-model="newTitle" value=""
                label="Title*" required></v-text-field>
            </v-flex>
```

```
                    <v-flex xs12 sm12 md12>
                        <v-textarea v-model="newContent" value=""
                        label="Content"></v-textarea>
                    </v-flex>
                </v-layout>
            </v-container>
            <small>*indicates required field</small>
        </v-card-text>
        <v-card-actions>
            <v-spacer></v-spacer>
            <v-btn color="blue darken-1" flat
            @click="closeModal()">Close</v-btn>
            <v-btn color="blue darken-1" flat
            @click="saveNote()">Save</v-btn>
        </v-card-actions>
    </v-card>
  </v-dialog>
  </v-app>
</template>

<script>
import Notes from './components/Notes.vue'

export default {
  name: 'app',
  components: {
    Notes
  },
  data: () => ({
    pages:[],
    newTitle: ",
    newContent: ",
```

```
    index:0,
    dialog: false
  }),
  methods:  {
    newNote () {
      this.dialog = true;
    },
    saveNote () {
      this.pages.push({
        title: this.newTitle,
        content: this.newContent
      });
      this.resetForm();
      this.closeModal();
    },
    closeModal () {
      this.dialog = false;
    },
    deleteNote () {

    },
    resetForm () {
      this.newTitle = ";
      this.newContent = ";
    }
  }
}
</script>
```

```
<style>
#app {
  font-family: 'Avenir', Helvetica, Arial, sans-serif;
  -webkit-font-smoothing: antialiased;
  -moz-osx-font-smoothing: grayscale;
  color: #2c3e50;
}
</style>
```

Notes.vue

```
<template>
  <div class="notes">
    <v-card v-for="(page, index) in pages" :key="index">
      <v-card-title primary-title>
        <div>
          <h3 class="headline mb-0">{{page.title}}</h3>
          <div>{{page.content}}</div>
        </div>
      </v-card-title>
    </v-card>
    <v-btn
      fab
      dark
      absolute
      right
      color="indigo"
      class="floatButton"
      @click="newNote()">
      <v-icon dark>add</v-icon>
    </v-btn>
  </div>
</template>
```

```
<script>
export default {
  name: 'Notes',
  props: ['pages'],
  methods: {
    newNote () {
    this.$emit('new-note');
    }
  }
}
</script>

<!-- Add "scoped" attribute to limit CSS to this component only
-->
<style scoped>
.floatButton {
  margin: 10px;
}
</style>
```

Now if you run our app, you can add notes, as shown in Figure 5-10.

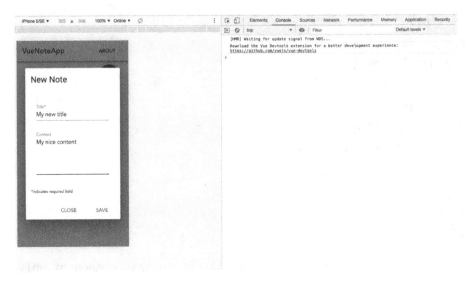

Figure 5-10. *Form to add a new note*

You can go there from the repo (`https://github.com/carlosrojaso/appress-book-pwa`) with

`$git checkout v1.1.2`

Deleting a Note

Users can now add notes in our app, but we also need to give them the ability to delete them as well. To do this, we need to modify our array pages where we keep our notes, remove the element that our user select to delete, and calculate the new size for our array. JS has two methods that can help us with this: `splice()` and `Math.max()`.

The `splice()` method allows us to change the content in our array. We use the `deleteNote(item)` method to pass the item index we want delete. We use `splice()` to remove it from the array.

```
deleteNote (item) {
      this.pages.splice( item, 1);
      ...
}
```

When we remove an item from the array, we need to update `this.index` data when we save the size of our `pages` array.

The `Math.max()` method allows us to get the largest value between values. We use it to avoid an error when we delete the last item. If we remove the last item, our index value will be –1, which results in unexpected behavior in our app. With `Math.max()`, we can assign a value of 0 to prevent this from happening.

```
deleteNote (item) {
    ...
    this.index = Math.max(this.index - 1, 0);
}
```

Challenge   Add an action button and accompanying functionality to our app to edit a note.

All the code together looks like this:

App.vue

```
<template>
  <v-app>
    <v-toolbar app>
      <v-toolbar-title >
        <span>VueNoteApp</span>
      </v-toolbar-title>
      <v-spacer></v-spacer>
      <v-toolbar-items>
        <v-btn flat>About</v-btn>
      </v-toolbar-items>
    </v-toolbar>
```

```
<v-content>
  <Notes :pages="pages" @new-note="newNote" @delete-
  note="deleteNote"/>
</v-content>
<v-dialog v-model="dialog">
<v-card>
  <v-card-title>
    <span class="headline">New Note</span>
  </v-card-title>
  <v-card-text>
    <v-container grid-list-md>
      <v-layout wrap>
        <v-flex xs12 sm12 md12>
          <v-text-field v-model="newTitle" value=""
          label="Title*" required></v-text-field>
        </v-flex>
        <v-flex xs12 sm12 md12>
          <v-textarea v-model="newContent" value=""
          label="Content"></v-textarea>
        </v-flex>
      </v-layout>
    </v-container>
    <small>*indicates required field</small>
  </v-card-text>
  <v-card-actions>
    <v-spacer></v-spacer>
    <v-btn color="blue darken-1" flat
    @click="closeModal()">Close</v-btn>
    <v-btn color="blue darken-1" flat
    @click="saveNote()">Save</v-btn>
  </v-card-actions>
```

```
    </v-card>
  </v-dialog>
  </v-app>
</template>

<script>
import Notes from './components/Notes.vue'

export default {
  name: 'app',
  components: {
    Notes
  },
  data: () => ({
    pages:[],
    newTitle: ",
    newContent: ",
    index: 0,
    dialog: false
  }),
  methods:  {
    newNote () {
      this.dialog = true;
    },
    saveNote () {
      this.pages.push({
        title: this.newTitle,
        content: this.newContent
      });
      this.index = this.pages.length - 1;
      this.resetForm();
      this.closeModal();
    },
```

```
    closeModal () {
      this.dialog = false;
    },
    deleteNote (item) {
      this.pages.splice( item, 1);
      this.index = Math.max(this.index - 1, 0);
    },
    resetForm () {
      this.newTitle = ";
      this.newContent = ";
    }
  }
}
</script>

<style>
#app {
  font-family: 'Avenir', Helvetica, Arial, sans-serif;
  -webkit-font-smoothing: antialiased;
  -moz-osx-font-smoothing: grayscale;
  color: #2c3e50;
}
</style>
```

Notes.vue

```
<template>
  <div class="notes">
    <v-card v-for="(page, index) in pages" :key="index">
      <v-card-title primary-title>
        <div>
          <h3 class="headline mb-0">{{page.title}}</h3>
          <div>{{page.content}}</div>
```

```
        </div>
      </v-card-title>
      <v-card-actions>
            <v-btn
            flat
            @click="deleteNote(index)"
            color="orange">Delete</v-btn>
      </v-card-actions>
    </v-card>
    <v-btn
      fab
      dark
      absolute
      right
      color="indigo"
      class="floatButton"
      @click="newNote()">
      <v-icon dark>add</v-icon>
    </v-btn>
  </div>
</template>

<script>
export default {
  name: 'Notes',
  props: ['pages'],
  methods: {
    newNote () {
    this.$emit('new-note');
    },
```

```
    deleteNote (item) {
    this.$emit('delete-note', item++);
    }
  }
}
</script>

<!-- Add "scoped" attribute to limit CSS to this component only
-->
<style scoped>
.floatButton {
  margin: 10px;
}
</style>
```

You can go there from the repo (https://github.com/carlosrojaso/appress-book-pwa) with

```
$git checkout v1.1.3
```

Check out Figure 5-11.

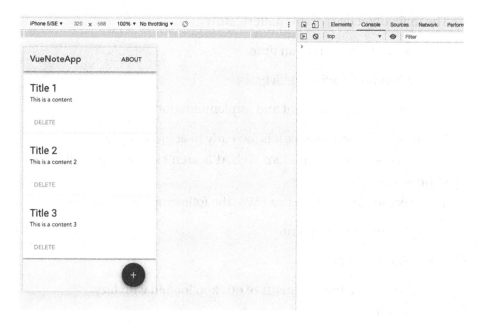

Figure 5-11.   *Delete button*

What Is the PRPL Architecture Pattern?

PRPL is an experimental web app architecture developed by Google for building web sites and apps that work exceptionally well with unreliable network connections.

PRPL stands for

- *Push* critical resources for the initial URL route.

- *Render* the initial route.

- *Precache* the remaining routes.

- *Lazy-load* and create remaining resources on demand.

The main objectives of this pattern are

- Minimum interaction time

- Maximum caching efficiency

- Making development and implementation easy

For most web app projects, it is too early to achieve all the PRPL requirements because the modern Web APIs aren't supported in all the major browsers.

To apply the PRPL pattern to a PWA, the following must be present:

- The main entry point

- The app shell

- The rest of the fragments of our app loaded with lazy loading

The Main Entry Point

The main entry point is in charge of loading the shell and any necessary polyfill[1] quickly. It also uses absolute paths for all its dependencies. In VueNoteApp, our main entry point is `index.html`.

The App Shell

The app shell is responsible for routing and includes minimal HTML and CSS code to interact with users as quickly as possible. In VueNoteApp, the app shell is generated with Workbox and is present in `precache-manifest.xxxxxx.js`, which is the name that is autogenerated each time we run `$npm run build`.

---

[1]`https://remysharp.com/2010/10/08/what-is-a-polyfill/`

Fragments Loaded with Lazy Loading

When building apps with a bundler, the JS bundle can become quite large, and thus affect page load time. It is more efficient if we split each route's components into separate chunks and then load them only when the route is visited.

We need to load one fragment on demand in our app when users click the About link. To do this, we develop an about view in About.vue, which looks something like this:

```
const About = () => import('./About.vue')
```

Then we add this new route to the router:

```
export const routes = [
  {path: ", component: HelloWorld},
  {path: '/about', component: About},
];
```

We add this to our app forward when we create our file routes.js, and delegate the lazy loading and bundle responsibility to Vue CLI.

The PRPL pattern is a paradigm designed to alleviate a stressful user experience while users browse the Web from their mobile device.

Adding a Router

Usually in our app, we switch between views. To do this, we need a routing mechanism. Vue.js has an official plug-in we need to add:

```
$npm install vue-router
```

We then follow the steps we took in the section "What Is a Vue Router?"

main.js

```
import Vue from 'vue'
import App from './App.vue'
import Vuetify from 'vuetify'
import VueRouter from 'vue-router'
import { routes } from "./routes"

import 'vuetify/dist/vuetify.min.css'
import './registerServiceWorker'

Vue.config.productionTip = false
Vue.use(Vuetify)
Vue.use(VueRouter);

const myRouter = new VueRouter({
  routes: routes
});

new Vue({
  router: myRouter,
  render: h => h(App),
}).$mount('#app')
```

We create a `routes.js` file to handle the router we are going to use
in our app. Something important here is that, if you remember the PRPL
pattern, we need to use lazy loading in our app. Here you can see that we
are loading `About.vue` in a lazy way:

routes.js

```
import Dashboard from './components/Dashboard.vue'
const lazyAbout = () => import('./components/About.vue')
```

```
export const routes = [
  {path: ", component: Dashboard},
  {path: '/dashboard', component: Dashboard},
  {path: '/about', component: lazyAbout}
];
```

All the code together looks like this:

App.vue

```
<template>
  <v-app>
    <v-toolbar app>
      <v-toolbar-title >
        <router-link to="/">VueNoteApp</router-link>
      </v-toolbar-title>
      <v-spacer></v-spacer>
      <v-toolbar-items>
        <v-btn
        to="/about"
        flat
        >About</v-btn>
      </v-toolbar-items>
    </v-toolbar>
    <router-view></router-view>
  </v-app>
</template>

<script>
export default {
  name: 'app'
}
</script>
```

```
<style>
#app {
  font-family: 'Avenir', Helvetica, Arial, sans-serif;
  -webkit-font-smoothing: antialiased;
  -moz-osx-font-smoothing: grayscale;
  color: #2c3e50;
}

a {
  text-decoration: none;
}
</style>
```

components/About.vue

```
<template>
  <div class="about">
    <v-content>
      <br/><b>Building PWAs with VueJS.</b><br/><br/>
      repo: https://github.com/carlosrojaso/appress-book-pwa<br/>
      2019
    </v-content>
  </div>
</template>

<script>
export default {
  name: 'About'
}
</script>
```

```
<!-- Add "scoped" attribute to limit CSS to this component only
-->
<style scoped>

</style>
```

components/Dashboard.vue

```
<template>
  <div class="dashboard">
    <v-content>
      <Notes :pages="pages" @new-note="newNote" @delete-
      note="deleteNote"/>
    </v-content>
    <v-dialog v-model="dialog">
        <v-card>
        <v-card-title>
            <span class="headline">New Note</span>
        </v-card-title>
        <v-card-text>
            <v-container grid-list-md>
            <v-layout wrap>
                <v-flex xs12 sm12 md12>
                <v-text-field v-model="newTitle" value=""
                label="Title*" required></v-text-field>
                </v-flex>
                <v-flex xs12 sm12 md12>
                <v-textarea v-model="newContent" value=""
                label="Content"></v-textarea>
                </v-flex>
            </v-layout>
            </v-container>
```

```
            <small>*indicates required field</small>
        </v-card-text>
        <v-card-actions>
            <v-spacer></v-spacer>
            <v-btn color="blue darken-1" flat
            @click="closeModal()">Close</v-btn>
            <v-btn color="blue darken-1" flat
            @click="saveNote()">Save</v-btn>
        </v-card-actions>
        </v-card>
    </v-dialog>
  </div>
</template>

<script>
import Notes from './Notes.vue'
export default {
  name: 'Dashboard',
  components: {
    Notes
  },
  data: () => ({
    pages:[],
    newTitle: ",
    newContent: ",
    index: 0,
    dialog: false
  }),
  methods: {
    newNote () {
      this.dialog = true;
    },
```

```
    saveNote () {
      this.pages.push({
        title: this.newTitle,
        content: this.newContent
      });
      this.index = this.pages.length - 1;
      this.resetForm();
      this.closeModal();
    },
    closeModal () {
      this.dialog = false;
    },
    deleteNote (item) {
      this.pages.splice( item, 1);
      this.index = Math.max(this.index - 1, 0);
    },
    resetForm () {
      this.newTitle = ";
      this.newContent = ";
    }
  }
}
</script>

<!-- Add "scoped" attribute to limit CSS to this component only -->
<style scoped>

</style>
```

components/Notes.vue

```
<template>
  <div class="notes">
    <v-card v-for="(page, index) in pages" :key="index">
      <v-card-title primary-title>
        <div>
          <h3 class="headline mb-0">{{page.title}}</h3>
          <div>{{page.content}}</div>
        </div>
      </v-card-title>
      <v-card-actions>
            <v-btn
            flat
            @click="deleteNote(index)"
            color="orange">Delete</v-btn>
      </v-card-actions>
    </v-card>
    <v-btn
      fab
      dark
      absolute
      right
      color="indigo"
      class="floatButton"
      @click="newNote()">
      <v-icon dark>add</v-icon>
    </v-btn>
  </div>
</template>
```

```
<script>
export default {
  name: 'Notes',
  props: ['pages'],
  methods: {
    newNote () {
    this.$emit('new-note');
    },
    deleteNote (item) {
    this.$emit('delete-note', item++);
    }
  }
}
</script>

<!-- Add "scoped" attribute to limit CSS to this component only
-->
<style scoped>
.floatButton {
  margin: 10px;
}
</style>
```

Now when we load our app, Vue.js just loads the resources for the main view, as shown in Figure 5-12.

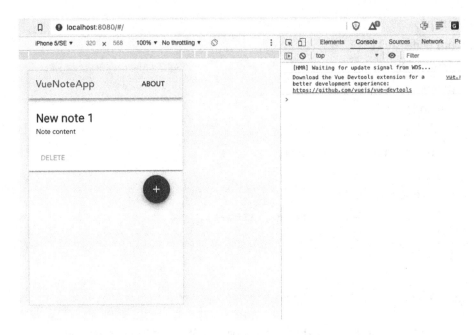

Figure 5-12. *VueNoteApp with router*

Other views, such as about, wait until the user navigates to the /about route to load that resource (Figure 5-13).

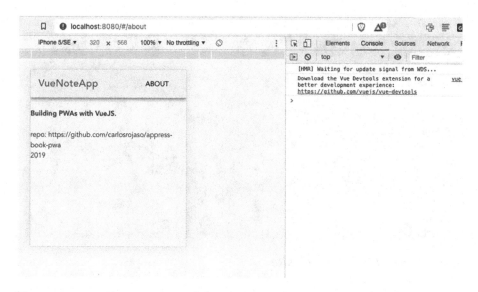

Figure 5-13. *VueNoteApp /about route*

As you can see in Figure 5-13, we have now an additional view. You can go there from the repo (`https://github.com/carlosrojaso/appress-book-pwa`) with

```
$git checkout v1.1.4
```

Adding Firebase

At this point, if we try to reload our app, we will see that we lost all our notes. Therefore, we need an external storage system that keeps our data and syncs them among all our clients.

Firebase Database is a perfect solution for syncing our data in real time to all our clients, and we can save the data easily with its JS software development kit.

To get started, sign in to `https://firebase.google.com/` and use your Google account to log in (Figure 5-14).

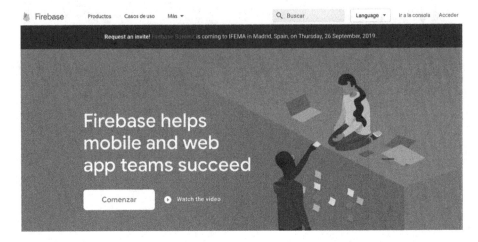

Figure 5-14. *Firebase web site*

Then go to the console (Figure 5-15).

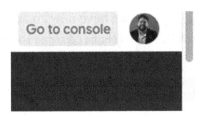

Figure 5-15. *Firebase console link*

We create a new project (as described in Chapter 1) and, in just minutes, we can start to use our new project (Figure 5-16).

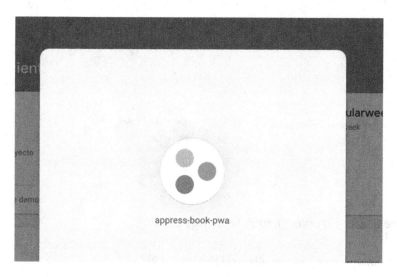

Figure 5-16. *Creating a new project*

When our project is ready in the Firebase console, we must provide information that allows us to connect our app and Firebase. Select Project Overview ➤ Project settings (Figure 5-17).

Figure 5-17. *Firebase project overview*

Select the web app button (the third button from the left in Figure 5-18).

Figure 5-18. *Firebase project settings view*

Firebase starts a setup wizard (Figure 5-19).

Figure 5-19. *Firebase web app wizard*

At the end, we see our `firebaseConfig` (Figure 5-20).

Figure 5-20. *Firebase configuration summary*

Copy this information.

The last thing we need to do in the console is to create a new database and open the security rules to be accessed without authentication (we do this to keep our app simple).

From Project Overview, select Database (Figure 5-21).

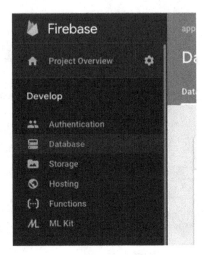

Figure 5-21. *Firebase Database link*

Then select Create Realtime Database (Figure 5-22).

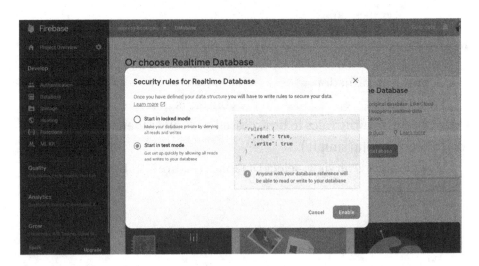

Figure 5-22. *Firebase security rules*

Make sure "Start in test mode" is selected. In this mode, we can write data to our database without having authentication. This is a handy feature during development, but it is unsafe during production. Now we can go back to our app.

In the terminal, run

```
$npm install firebase --save
```

Then, create a new file—firebase.js—and paste in the data from your Firebase project.

firebase.js

```
import Firebase from 'firebase';

let config = {
  apiKey: "AIzaSyDT2_jZiasDKO17UicoakK1gn93FIZnJ5o",
  authDomain: "appress-book-pwa.firebaseapp.com",
  databaseURL: "https://appress-book-pwa.firebaseio.com",
  projectId: "appress-book-pwa",
  storageBucket: "",
  messagingSenderId: "217988350403",
  appId: "1:217988350403:web:cd5e278739086fd1"
};

export const app = Firebase.initializeApp(config);
```

Next, import in main.js.

main.js

```
import './firebase';

import Vue from 'vue'
import App from './App.vue'
import Vuetify from 'vuetify'
import VueRouter from 'vue-router'
import { routes } from "./routes"

...
```

Now, in `Dashboard.vue`, we need to use the life cycle method `mounted()` to recover all the notes in our real-time database. We also need to update `saveNote()` and `deleteNote()` to update the new notes in Firebase.

We import `fireApp` from `firebase.js` to keep a reference in our app with

```
const db = fireApp.database().ref();
```

With `db.push`, we can add data to Firebase; with `remove()`, we can delete data from Firebase. For more information, go to `https://firebase.google.com/docs/reference/js/firebase.database`.

Dashboard.vue

```
<template>
  <div class="dashboard">
    <v-content>
      <Notes :pages="pages" @new-note="newNote" @delete-
      note="deleteNote"/>
    </v-content>
    <v-dialog v-model="dialog">
        <v-card>
        <v-card-title>
            <span class="headline">New Note</span>
        </v-card-title>
        <v-card-text>
            <v-container grid-list-md>
            <v-layout wrap>
                <v-flex xs12 sm12 md12>
                <v-text-field v-model="newTitle" value=""
                label="Title*" required></v-text-field>
                </v-flex>
```

```
                <v-flex xs12 sm12 md12>
                <v-textarea v-model="newContent" value=""
                label="Content"></v-textarea>
                </v-flex>
            </v-layout>
            </v-container>
            <small>*indicates required field</small>
        </v-card-text>
        <v-card-actions>
            <v-spacer></v-spacer>
            <v-btn color="blue darken-1" flat
            @click="closeModal()">Close</v-btn>
            <v-btn color="blue darken-1" flat
            @click="saveNote()">Save</v-btn>
        </v-card-actions>
        </v-card>
    </v-dialog>
  </div>
</template>

<script>
import {fireApp} from'../firebase.js'
import Notes from './Notes.vue'

const db = fireApp.database().ref();

export default {
  name: 'Dashboard',
  components: {
    Notes
  },
```

```
data: () => ({
  pages:[],
  newTitle: ",
  newContent: ",
  index: 0,
  dialog: false
}),
mounted() {
  db.once('value', (notes) => {
    notes.forEach((note) => {
      this.pages.push({
        title: note.child('title').val(),
        content: note.child('content').val(),
        ref: note.ref
      })
    })
  })
},
methods:  {
  newNote () {
    this.dialog = true;
  },
  saveNote () {
    const newItem = {
      title: this.newTitle,
      content: this.newContent
    };
    this.pages.push(newItem);
    this.index = this.pages.length - 1;
    db.push(newItem);
```

```
      this.resetForm();
      this.closeModal();
    },
    closeModal () {
      this.dialog = false;
    },
    deleteNote (item) {
      let noteRef = this.pages[item].ref;
      if(noteRef) { noteRef.remove(); }
      this.pages.splice( item, 1);
      this.index = Math.max(this.index - 1, 0);
    },
    resetForm () {
      this.newTitle = ";
      this.newContent = ";
    }
  }
}
</script>

<!-- Add "scoped" attribute to limit CSS to this component only -->
<style scoped>

</style>
```

Now we should be able to see our data store in Firebase (Figure 5-23).

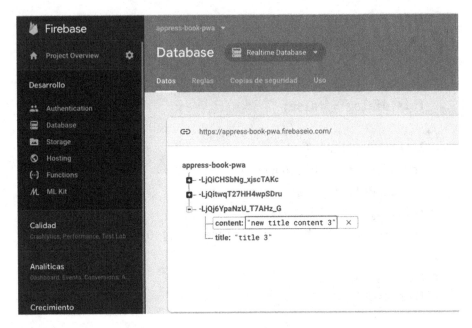

Figure 5-23. *Firebase Database console*

And when we refresh our data, they are saved (Figure 5-24).

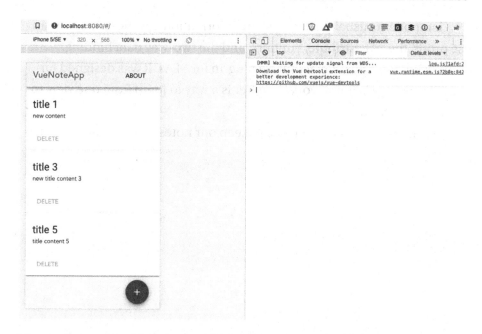

Figure 5-24. *VueNoteApp with the data in Firebase*

You can go there from the repo (`https://github.com/carlosrojaso/appress-book-pwa`) with

```
$git checkout v1.1.5
```

Summary

The core library of Vue.js is focused on the view layer only, and it is easy to pick up and integrate with other libraries or existing projects.

Components are created and destroyed during their life cycle, and there are methods we can use to run functions at specific times. These methods are called *life cycle hooks*. Life cycle hooks are an essential part of any serious component.

Components usually need to share information. To effect this, we can use props, the `ref` attribute, emitters, and the two-way data binding.

Vue Router is an official routing plug-in for SPAs. It was designed for use with the Vue.js framework. A router is a way to jump from one view to another in an SPA.

We can use Firebase Database to keep our notes synced among all the clients.

CHAPTER 6

IndexedDB

At some point in our development, we want to save transactional information when our app is offline. We could save it in cache storage, but this can be complex, such as in scenarios like managing the information in a CRUD (Create, Read, Update, Remove). To help in these instances, we have technology that has existed in web browsers for a very long time: IndexedDB.

What Is IndexedDB?

IndexedDB is a transactional database system that, unlike other options that we have in browsers, is perfect for storing significant amounts of data, such as catalogs or other types that require a quick information search. Some terms with which to familiarize yourself about IndexedDB are as follows:

- *Object store*: Object stores are similar to tables or relations in traditional relational databases.

- *Database*: Databases are where all the object stores are kept. You can create as many databases as you want, but usually one per app is sufficient.

© Carlos Rojas 2020
C. Rojas, *Building Progressive Web Applications with Vue.js*,
https://doi.org/10.1007/978-1-4842-5334-2_6

- *Transaction*: Every action in IndexedDB works through a transaction. To effect any action, you first need to create a transaction, then listen for events on completion. Transactions are useful for maintaining integrity. If one of the operations fails, the whole action is canceled.

One feature that makes IndexedDB perfect to be used with PWAs is that it is asynchronous. Previously, it was both synchronous and asynchronous. The synchronous API was intended for use only with web workers, but was removed from the spec because it was unclear whether it was needed. For more information on the asynchronous API, see `https://developer.mozilla.org/en-US/docs/Web/API/IndexedDB_API/Using_IndexedDB`.

Using IndexedDB

In general terms, the process of using IndexedDB with our app is shown in Figure 6-1.

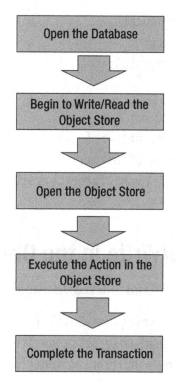

Figure 6-1. *IndexedDB workflow*

Opening a DB

The process to open IndexedDB using JS is as follows:

```
var connection;
connection = window.indexedDB.open("notes", 1);

connection.onsuccess = (event) => {
// data
let dummyData = [];
```

```
// Opening successful process.
db = event.target.result;
writingObjectStore(dummyData);
readingObjectStore();
};

connection.onerror = (event) => {
// We handle the opening DB error.
console.error('error:', event.target.errorCode);
};
```

Initiating Read/Write in the Object Store

The proccess to write/read from IndexedDB using JS is as follows:

```
function writingObjectStore(dummyData) {
        // It can be read-only or readwrite.
        var transaction = db.transaction(['notes'], 'readwrite');

        // Adding the data in objectStore.
        let objectStore = transaction.objectStore("notes");
        dummyData.forEach(
            (note) => {
            let request = objectStore.add(note);

            request.onerror = (e) => {
              // Handle the error.
            };
            request.onsuccess = (e) => {
                console.log('Item added to indexedDB');
            };
            }
        );
}
```

```
function readingObjectStore() {
        let transaction = db.transaction(["notes"], "readonly");
        // Adding the data in objectStore.
        let objectStore = transaction.objectStore('notes') ;
        let request = objectStore.getAll();
        request.onsuccess = () => {
            request.result.forEach((item) => console.log('Items
            by name:', item));
            };
}
```

Deleting from the Object Store

The process to delete from IndexedDB using JS is as follows:

```
function deletingFromTheObjectStore() {
        // Deleting a registry.
        let request = db.transaction(["notes"], "readwrite")
                            .objectStore("notes")
                            .delete("title 1");
        request.onsuccess = (event) => {
                // It was deleted successfully.
                console.log('registry deleted');
            };
}
```

All the code together looks like this:

```
<script>
    (function() {
    var db;
    var connection;
```

```
connection = window.indexedDB.open("notes", 1);

connection.onupgradeneeded = (upgradeDb) => {
    var db = upgradeDb.target.result;
    if (!db.objectStoreNames.contains('notes')) {
        db.createObjectStore('notes', {keyPath: 'title'});
    }
};

connection.onsuccess = (event) => {
// data
let dummyData = [
{
"title": "title 1",
"content": "PWA"
},
{
"title": "title 2",
"content": "Loren Ipsum"
}
];

// Opening successful process.
db = event.target.result;

writingObjectStore(dummyData);
readingObjectStore();
};

connection.onerror = (event) => {
// We handle the opening DB error.
console.error('error:', event.target.errorCode);
};
```

```
function writingObjectStore(dummyData) {
    // It can be read-only or readwrite.
    var transaction = db.transaction(['notes'], 'readwrite');

    // Adding the data in objectStore.
    let objectStore = transaction.objectStore("notes");
    dummyData.forEach(
        (note) => {
        let request = objectStore.add(note);

        request.onerror = (e) => {
        };
        request.onsuccess = (e) => {
            console.log('Item added to indexedDB');
        };
        }
    );
}

function readingObjectStore() {
    let transaction = db.transaction(["notes"], "readonly");
    // Adding the data in objectStore.
    let objectStore = transaction.objectStore('notes') ;
    let request = objectStore.getAll();
    request.onsuccess = () => {
        request.result.forEach((item) => console.log('Items
        by name:', item));
        };
}
```

```
function deletingFromTheObjectStore() {
    // Deleting a registry.
    let request = db.transaction(["notes"], "readwrite")
                    .objectStore("notes")
                    .delete("title 1");
    request.onsuccess = (event) => {
        // It was deleted successfully.
        console.log('registry deleted');
    };
}

})();
</script>
```

You can go there from the repo (https://github.com/carlosrojaso/appress-book-pwa) with

```
$git checkout indexedDB-plain
$serve -S indexedDB
```

Run the server, In your browser open Chrome DevTools and now you can see the same like in Figure 6-2.

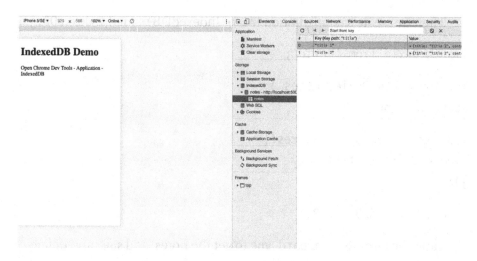

Figure 6-2. Using IndexedDB with plain JS

Using IndexedDB in VueNoteApp

As you can see, using IndexedDB is relatively easy, but at some point it can get messy with regard to design and implementation. This is the reason why there are libraries and wrappers that help us handle transactions more easily. I recommend localForage (similar to localStorage), but my favorite is Dexie.js. I like it because it allows me to use promises easily and is well documented. You can find the documentation at `https://dexie.org/docs/`.

To work with Dexie.js, we have to move to a new branch of IndexedDB in git:

```
$git checkout indexedDB
```

And we need to install Dexie.js in our project:

```
$npm install dexie --save
```

Then we create a configuration file for IndexedDB named `indexedDB.js`:

```
import Dexie from 'dexie';

let iDB = new Dexie('Notes');
const version = 1;

iDB.version(version).stores({
  notes: '++id, title'
});

export let indDB = iDB;
```

Later, we update `Dashboard.vue` to get the notes, and save and delete from IndexedDB:

```
<template>
  <div class="dashboard">
    <v-content>
      <Notes :pages="pages" @new-note="newNote"
      @delete-note="deleteNote"/>
    </v-content>
    <v-dialog v-model="dialog">
        <v-card>
        <v-card-title>
            <span class="headline">New Note</span>
        </v-card-title>
        <v-card-text>
            <v-container grid-list-md>
            <v-layout wrap>
                <v-flex xs12 sm12 md12>
                <v-text-field v-model="newTitle" value=""
                label="Title*" required></v-text-field>
                </v-flex>
```

```
            <v-flex xs12 sm12 md12>
            <v-textarea v-model="newContent" value=""
            label="Content"></v-textarea>
            </v-flex>
        </v-layout>
        </v-container>
        <small>*indicates required field</small>
    </v-card-text>
    <v-card-actions>
        <v-spacer></v-spacer>
        <v-btn color="blue darken-1" flat
        @click="closeModal()">Close</v-btn>
        <v-btn color="blue darken-1" flat
        @click="saveNote()">Save</v-btn>
    </v-card-actions>
    </v-card>
  </v-dialog>
 </div>
</template>

<script>
import {indDB} from '../indexedDB.js'
import Notes from './Notes.vue'

export default {
  name: 'Dashboard',
  components: {
    Notes
  },
```

```
data: () => ({
  pages:[],
  newTitle: ",
  newContent: ",
  index: 0,
  dialog: false
}),
mounted() {
  indDB.open().catch(function (e) {
    console.log("Something happened opening indexed DB:
    " + e.stack);
  });
  this.getAllRows();
},
methods:  {
  newNote () {
    this.dialog = true;
  },
  saveNote () {
    const newItem = {
      title: this.newTitle,
      content: this.newContent
    };
    this.pages.push(newItem);
    this.index = this.pages.length - 1;

    indDB.transaction('rw',indDB.notes,() =>
    {
      indDB.notes.add(newItem);
    });
```

```
      this.resetForm();
      this.closeModal();
    },
    closeModal () {
      this.dialog = false;
    },
    getAllRows () {
      indDB.notes.each(note => {this.pages.push(note);});
    },
    deleteNote (item) {
      this.deleteRow(this.pages[item]);
      this.pages.splice( item, 1);
      this.index = Math.max(this.index - 1, 0);
    },
    deleteRow (item){
      const criteria = {'title': item.title};
      // Get primaryKey.
      indDB.notes.where(criteria).first(
        (result) => {
          indDB.notes.delete(result.id);
        }
      );
    },
    resetForm () {
      this.newTitle = ";
      this.newContent = ";
    }
  }
}
</script>
```

```
<!-- Add "scoped" attribute to limit CSS to this component only
-->
<style scoped>

</style>
```

You can check the IndexedDB database in Chrome DevTools in the Application tab (Figure 6-3).

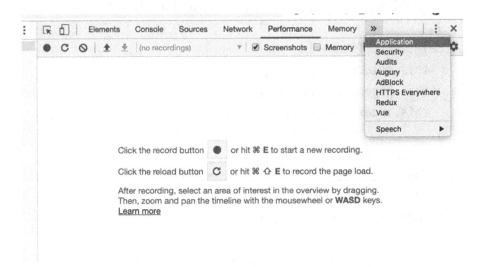

Figure 6-3. *Chrome DevTools Application tab*

From the Application tab, select Storage ➤ IndexedDB. You should see something like what is presented in Figure 6-4.

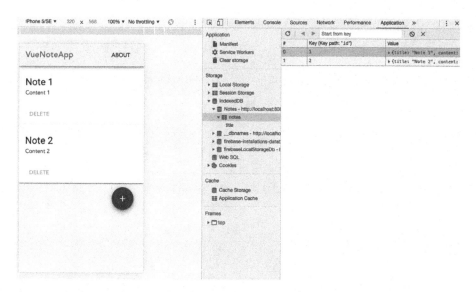

Figure 6-4. *Chrome DevTools IndexedDB storage view*

Summary

IndexedDB is a transactional database system that is perfect for storing significant amounts of data, which makes it a good choice to use for our app.

CHAPTER 7

Background Sync

There are scenarios when our users expect an app to react automatically during disconnection. If they do something in the app while they are offline, the system resumes the state when a connection is available. In these cases, Background Sync is useful to us.

Think, for a second, about a chat app. As a user, I hope that, if I have a few spare seconds, I can see the messages I get from friends and have time to answer each message, close the app, then continue on with my life. However, what if I'm in a place with flaky or no connectivity? I probably can't answer the messages because, if I try, a blank page or a loader or an error message will show up (if I'm using a regular web app). However, with Background Sync in our PWA, users can answer messages and let the app handle them when connection returns to the device.

Using Background Sync

Background Sync, combined with a service worker, grants us great power in building PWAs. Using Background Sync is relatively easy. We simply register our event with SyncManager and react to the sync event:

```
navigator.serviceWorker.ready
.then(function(registration){
        registration.sync.register('my-event-sync');
});
```

© Carlos Rojas 2020
C. Rojas, *Building Progressive Web Applications with Vue.js*,
https://doi.org/10.1007/978-1-4842-5334-2_7

After we register our event, we can use it from our service worker in the sync event:

```
self.addEventListener("sync",
function(event) {
        if (event.tag === "my-event-sync") {
        // The logic of our event goes here.
        }
}
);
```

SyncManager

SyncManager is the service worker API that handles and registers synchronized events (Figure 7-1).

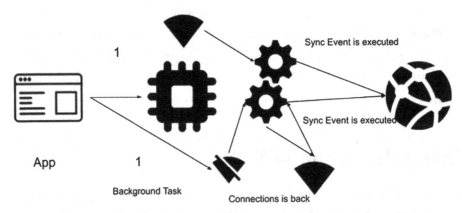

Figure 7-1. *SyncManager workflow*

A sync event is triggered when

- A sync event is registered

- When the user goes from offline to online

- Every few minutes if there is a registry that has not been completed successfully

To work with SyncManager, we use three things: the event tags, the getTags() method, and the lastChance() method.

Event Tags

The event tags allow us to register events in SyncManager. They are unique and, if they are repeated, SyncManager ignores them.

```
self.addEventListener('sync', function(event) {
 cont tag = event.tag
});
```

Obtaining the Event List

We can obtain all registered events in SyncManager using the getTags() method, which returns a promise:

```
navigator.serviceWorker.ready.then(
 (registration) => {
 registration.sync.getTags().then((tag)=> console.log(tag));
 }
);
```

Obtaining the Last Chance of an Event

In some cases, SyncManager decides to discard an event that has failed multiple times. However, when this occurs, SyncManager allows you to react to this event using the lastChance() method:

```
self.addEventListener('sync', function(event) {
 console.log('I am in sync', event.tag);
 if(event.lastChance) {
 // Do something; last opportunity.
 }
});
```

As you can see, Background Sync is pretty easy to use, and it opens an infinite world of possibilities to add a positive experience for our users. Also, we can mix it with IndexedDB and make our apps more reliable. Continuing with the chat app example I mentioned at the beginning of the chapter, we can do something like this:

index.html

```
<!DOCTYPE html>
<html lang="en">
<head>
 <meta charset="UTF-8">
 <meta name="viewport" content="width=device-width, initial-
 scale=1.0">
 <meta http-equiv="X-UA-Compatible" content="ie=edge">
 <title>Background Sync</title>
</head>
<body>
 <h1>Background Sync Demo</h1>
 <p>Open Chrome Dev Tools</p>
 <button id="myButton">Send Message</button>
 <script>
 if ('serviceWorker' in navigator) {
 // Register a service worker hosted at the root of the
 // site using a more restrictive scope.
 navigator.serviceWorker.register('/sw.js', {scope: './'}).
 then(
 (registration) => {
 console.log('Service worker registration succeeded:',
 registration);
 },
```

```
(error) => {
console.log('Service worker registration failed:', error);
}
);
} else {
console.log('Service workers are not supported.');
}
</script>
<script src="./indexedDB.js"></script>
<script src="./app.js"></script>
</body>
</html>
```

Next, we simulate a chat app. We add reliability by saving messages in a queue in IndexedDB, then send some messages to a fake API (see https://jsonplaceholder.typicode.com/guide.html for more information). When the response is successful, we delete the messages from the queue; otherwise, we try sending them later with Background Sync (Figure 7-2).

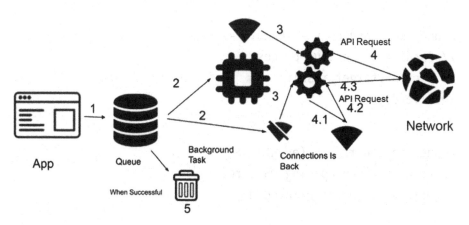

Figure 7-2. *Chat app workflow*

We need a basic IndexedDB implementation to handle the queue logic.

indexedDB.js

```
var DB_VERSION = 1;
var DB_NAME = "messages";
var db;
var connection;

function openDatabase(){
 return new Promise(
 (resolve, reject) => {
 connection = self.indexedDB.open(DB_NAME, DB_VERSION);

 connection.onupgradeneeded = (upgradeDb) => {
 var db = upgradeDb.target.result;
 if (!db.objectStoreNames.contains('message-queue')) {
 db.createObjectStore('message-queue', {keyPath: 'title'});
 }
 };

 connection.onsuccess = (event) => {
 // Opening successful process.
 db = event.target.result;
 resolve(db);
 };

 connection.onerror = (event) => {
 // We handle the opening DB error.
 reject(event.target.errorCode);
 };
 }
 );
}
```

```javascript
function writingObjectStore(data) {
 // It can be read-only or readwrite.
 var transaction = db.transaction(['message-queue'],
'readwrite');

 // Adding the data in objectStore.
 let objectStore = transaction.objectStore("message-queue");

 let request = objectStore.add(data);

 request.onerror = (e) => {
 };
 request.onsuccess = (e) => {
 console.log('Item added to indexedDB');
 };
}

function getAllMessagesFromQueue() {
 return new Promise(
 (resolve, reject) => {
 let transaction = db.transaction(["message-queue"],
 "readonly");
 // Adding the data in objectStore.
 let objectStore = transaction.objectStore('message-queue') ;
 let request = objectStore.getAll();
 request.onsuccess = () => {
 resolve(request.result);
 };
 request.onerror = () => {
 reject(request.error);
 }
 }
 );
}
```

```
function deleteMessageFromQueue(item) {
 console.log('deleteMessageFromQueue()');
 return new Promise(
 (resolve, reject) => {
 // Deleting a registry.
 let request = db.transaction(["message-queue"], "readwrite")
 .objectStore("message-queue")
 .delete(item.title);
 request.onsuccess = () => {
 // It was deleted successfully.
 console.log('message deleted', item);
 resolve(request.result);
 };
 request.onerror = () => {
 // It was deleted successfully.
 reject(request.error);
 };
 }
 );
}
```

Next we add the sync event to our service worker.

sw.js

```
importScripts("/indexedDB.js");
const url = 'https://jsonplaceholder.typicode.com';

self.addEventListener('install', function(event) {
 // Perform install steps.
});

self.addEventListener('sync', function(event) {
 console.log('I am in sync', event.tag);
```

```
 if(event.tag === 'message-queue') {
 event.waitUntil(syncMessages());
 }
});

function syncMessages() {
 console.log('syncMessages()');
 openDatabase()
 .then(() => {
 getAllMessagesFromQueue()
 .then((messages) => {
 console.log('messages', messages);
 solveMessages(messages);
 });
 })
 .catch((e)=>{console.log(e)});
}

function solveMessages(messages) {
 Promise.all(
 messages.map(
 (message) => {
 console.log('a message', message);
 fetch(`${url}/posts`,
 {
 method: 'post',
 body: JSON.stringify({
 title: message.title,
 body: message.body,
 userId: message.userId
 }),
```

```
  headers: {
  "Content-type": "application/json; charset=UTF-8"
  }
  }
  )
  .then((response) => {
  console.log('response>>>', response);
  return deleteMessageFromQueue(message);
  });
  }
  )
  )

}
```

In the service worker in the previous code, note the inclusion of `importScripts()` (for more information, go to `https://developer.mozilla.org/en-US/docs/Web/API/WorkerGlobalScope/importScripts`). With it, we can find libraries and other scripts in the service worker scope—in our case, the `indexedDB.js` script. We separate our code using `syncMessages()`, where we get all the messages in our queue, then call to `solveMessages()`, where we use `fetch()` to make a request to our API. If this call is successful, we delete the messages from our queue.

Last, we need to add functionality to our app.

App.js

```
let button = document.getElementById('myButton');

const messagesToSend = [
  {
  title: 'new Message',
  body: 'Hello there',
  userId: 1
```

```
  },
  {
  title: 'new Message 2',
  body: 'Hello there again',
  userId: 1
  },
  {
  title: 'new Message 3',
  body: 'Hello there again again',
  userId: 1
  },
  {
  title: 'new Message 4',
  body: 'Hello there again 4 times',
  userId: 1
  }
];

button.addEventListener('click', function(){
 messagesToSend.forEach(
 (item) => {
 sendMessage(item);
 }
 );
 messageQueueSync();
});

// Background Sync Mechanism Functions

function sendMessage(message) {
 let messageItem = {
 title: message.title,
```

```
 body: message.body,
 userId: message.userId
 };

 openDatabase()
 .then(() => {
 writingObjectStore(messageItem);
 })
 .catch((e)=>{console.log(e)});

}


function messageQueueSync() {
 navigator.serviceWorker.ready.then(
 (registration) => {
 registration.sync.register('message-queue');
 }
 );
}
```

In the previous code, we simulated sending four messages and continuing the process with our queue (Figure 7-3).

You can go there from the repo (https://github.com/carlosrojaso/ appress-book-pwa) with

```
$ git checkout backgroundSync-plain
$ serve -S indexedDB
```

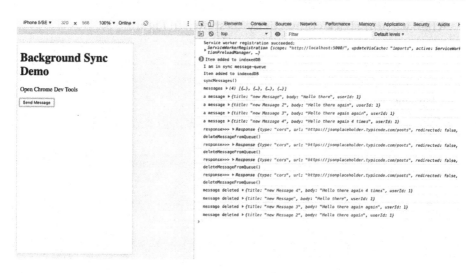

Figure 7-3. *Simulating chat messages online*

Now we can simulate an offline chat by selecting the Offline check box from the Service Workers panel (Figure 7-4).

Figure 7-4. *Simulating chat messages offline*

Then we bring back connectivity, as shown in Figure 7-5.

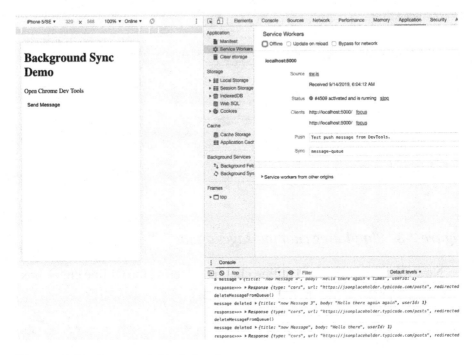

Figure 7-5. *Connectivity is back*

Using Background Sync in VueNoteApp

Workbox makes it easy for us to implement Background Sync in our
service worker. We need only modify our `src/service-worker.js` file
and add `workbox.backgroundSync.Plugin()` (for more information, go
to `https://developers.google.com/web/tools/workbox/modules/`
`workbox-background-sync`).

service-worker.js

```
workbox.setConfig({ debug: true });

const showNotification = () => {
 self.registration.showNotification('Sync success!', {
 body: 'Queue Resolved `🎊`'
 });
};

const bgSyncPlugin = new workbox.backgroundSync.
Plugin('myQueue', {
 maxRetentionTime: 24 * 60, // Retry for max of 24 Hours
 (specified in minutes)
 callbacks: {
 queueDidReplay: showNotification
 }
});

const networkWithBackgroundSync = new workbox.strategies.
NetworkOnly({
 plugins: [bgSyncPlugin],
});

workbox.routing.registerRoute(/\/*/, networkWithBackgroundSync,
"POST");
```

Now let's create a notification that shows up when all the pending POST requests are resolved, which is handled by workbox.backgroundSync. Plugin() in the queueDidReplay callback.

In addition, we need to use the NetworkOnly() method because our API request call and and we are using workbox.routing. registerRoute(/\/*/, networkWithBackgroundSync, "POST"); to catch all the POST calls.

Then we add addtoApiNote() in Dashboard.vue to simulate a call to an API.

Dashboard.vue

```
<template>
 <div class="dashboard">
 <v-content>
 <Notes :pages="pages" @new-note="newNote"
 @delete-note="deleteNote"/>
 </v-content>
 <v-dialog v-model="dialog">
 <v-card>
 <v-card-title>
 <span class="headline">New Note</span>
 </v-card-title>
 <v-card-text>
 <v-container grid-list-md>
 <v-layout wrap>
 <v-flex xs12 sm12 md12>
 <v-text-field v-model="newTitle" value="" label="Title*"
 required></v-text-field>
 </v-flex>
 <v-flex xs12 sm12 md12>
 <v-textarea v-model="newContent" value="" label="Content">
 </v-textarea>
 </v-flex>
 </v-layout>
 </v-container>
 <small>*indicates required field</small>
 </v-card-text>
 <v-card-actions>
```

```
<v-spacer></v-spacer>
<v-btn color="blue darken-1" flat @
click="closeModal()">Close</v-btn>
<v-btn color="blue darken-1" flat @click="saveNote()">Save
</v-btn>
</v-card-actions>
</v-card>
</v-dialog>
</div>
</template>

<script>
import {fireApp} from'../firebase.js'
import Notes from './Notes.vue'

const db = fireApp.database().ref();

export default {
 name: 'Dashboard',
 components: {
 Notes
 },
 data: () => ({
 pages:[],
 newTitle: ",
 newContent: ",
 index: 0,
 dialog: false
 }),
 mounted() {
 db.once('value', (notes) => {
 notes.forEach((note) => {
 this.pages.push({
```

```
    title: note.child('title').val(),
    content: note.child('content').val(),
    ref: note.ref
  })
})
})
},
methods: {
  newNote () {
    this.dialog = true;
  },
  saveNote () {
    const newItem = {
      title: this.newTitle,
      content: this.newContent
    };
    this.pages.push(newItem);
    this.index = this.pages.length - 1;
    db.push(newItem);
    this.addtoAPINote(newItem);
    this.resetForm();
    this.closeModal();
  },
  addtoAPINote(note) {
    fetch('https://jsonplaceholder.typicode.com/posts',
    {
      method: 'POST',
      body: JSON.stringify({
        title: note.title,
        body: note.body,
        userId: 1
      }),
```

```
headers: {
"Content-type": "application/json; charset=UTF-8"
}
}
).then(
(response) => {
// eslint-disable-next-line
console.log('fetch call:', response);
}
).catch(
() => {
// eslint-disable-next-line
console.log('Error sending to API...');
}
);
},
closeModal () {
this.dialog = false;
},
deleteNote (item) {
let noteRef = this.pages[item].ref;
if(noteRef) { noteRef.remove(); }
this.pages.splice( item, 1);
this.index = Math.max(this.index - 1, 0);
},
resetForm () {
this.newTitle = ";
this.newContent = ";
}
}
}
</script>
```

```
<!-- Add "scoped" attribute to limit CSS to this component only
-->
<style scoped>

</style>
```

With this method, when someone adds a note, the app makes an API call (Figure 7-6). You can go there from the repo (`https://github.com/carlosrojaso/appress-book-pwa`) with

```
$ git checkout backgroundSync
$ npm run build
$ serve -S dist
```

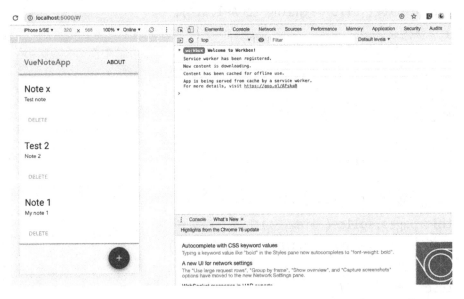

Figure 7-6. *Cleaning and rerunning our app with Background Sync enabled*

Next we need to go to Chrome DevTools ➤ Application ➤ Background Sync and activate recording Background Sync (Figure 7-7).

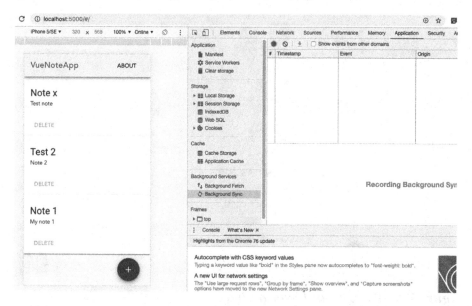

Figure 7-7. *Activating recording Background Sync activity in Chrome DevTools*

Now we need to turn off the computer network (Figure 7-8).

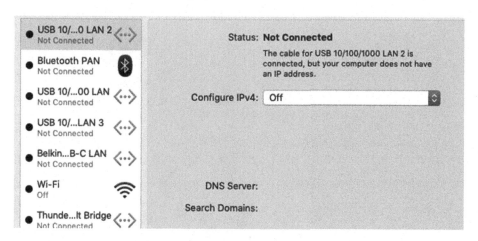

Figure 7-8. *Turning off networking in OS X*

Now try to add a note (Figure 7-9).

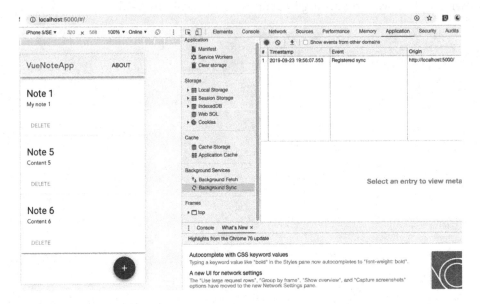

Figure 7-9. *Background Sync activity*

Figure 7-10 shows that Background Sync detects that the API calls were unsuccessful and saves then in IndexedDB.

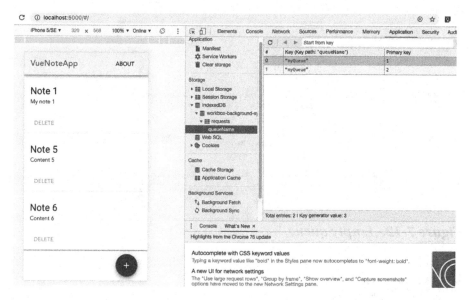

Figure 7-10. *IndexedDB queue*

Now let's turn on the computer network (Figure 7-11).

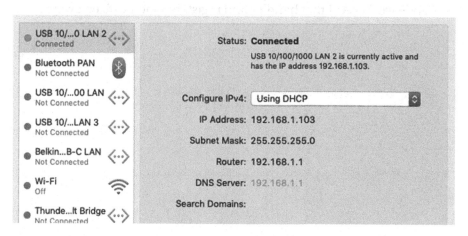

Figure 7-11. *Turning on networking in OS X*

Figure 7-12 shows the notification and the empty queue.

Figure 7-12. *Empty queue*

Summary

Background Sync, combined with a service worker, grants us the ability to build PWAs. Using Background Sync is relatively easy. We simply register our event with SyncManager and react to the sync event. SyncManager is the service worker API that handles and registers synchronized events.

CHAPTER 8

Push Notifications

One of the reasons why I think that service workers are starting to be used in web apps is to add the push notifications capability (Figure 8-1).

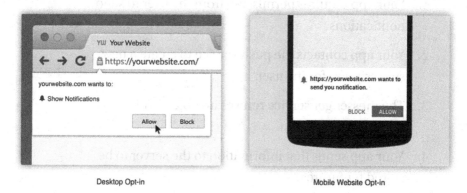

Desktop Opt-in   Mobile Website Opt-in

Figure 8-1. *Allowing push notifications in web and mobile devices*

Having push notifications allows us to interact with our users even when they have closed our app. This is common in the mobile world, but inside the web world, it was something that could not be achieved easily until now.

C. Rojas, *Building Progressive Web Applications with Vue.js*,
https://doi.org/10.1007/978-1-4842-5334-2_8

What Is a Push Notification?

Think, for a moment, about your chat app on your mobile phone. When you use the app, you can see messages and notifications when people write to you. However, what happens when you aren't using the app? Although the app is closed, the notification is "pushed" to you without you needing to do anything, and you see it in the notification center.

Technically speaking, a push notification is basically an interaction that includes a push API and a notification API.

Here is the sequence:

1. Your app requires permission from the user to send notifications.

2. Your app contacts the push service to create a new subscription for the user.

3. The messenger service returns an object with relevant information.

4. Your app sends that information to the server to be stored for future use.

5. The server sends messages to the user with the stored information.

6. The service worker listens to the messages.

7. The service worker notifies the user of the message.

Push API

The push API gives your app the capacity to receive push messages sent from a server. As mentioned previously, for an app to receive push messages, it must have an active service worker. Thanks to the active service worker, we can use `PushManager.subscribe()` to allow users to subscribe to our service notifications.

A general use example is as follows:

```
navigator.serviceWorker.register(sw.js').then(
  (serviceWorkerRegistration) => {
    var options = {
      userVisibleOnly: true,
      applicationServerKey: applicationServerKey
    };
    serviceWorkerRegistration.pushManager.subscribe(options).
    then(
      function(pushSubscription) => {
        console.log(pushSubscription.endpoint);
      }
    );
});
```

When using `applicationServerKey` (a token we get from our back end or a service such as Firebase Cloud Messaging), we allow user subscription. If you want to know more details about the push API, go to `https://www.w3.org/TR/push-api/`.

Notifications API

The notifications API allows an app to show a system notification even if the app is closed by the user (Figure 8-2).

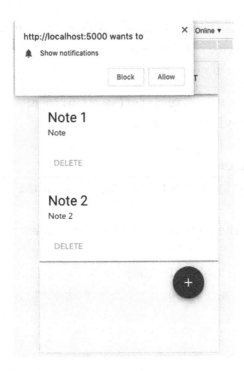

Figure 8-2. *Notifications API*

Asking for Permission

If our app has the capacity to send push notifications, the first thing we must do is ask permission from the user to send them. To handle this scenario, we create the following function:

```
function showMe() {
  if (!("Notification" in window)) {
    console.log("Does not support notifications");
  }
  else if (Notification.permission === "granted") {
      new Notification("Hello World!");
  }
```

```
else if (Notification.permission !== 'denied') {
    Notification.requestPermission(function (permission) {
        if (permission === "granted") {
        new Notification("Hello World!");

    }
  });
 }
}
```

With this function, we are ready to handle the permission action from our users.

Creating a Notification

We can create a function using the Notification() builder, which allows us to generate notifications easily in the following way:

```
function createNotification(theBody,theIcon,theTitle) {
  var options = {
      body: theBody,
      icon: theIcon
  }
  var n = new Notification(theTitle,options);
  setTimeout(n.close.bind(n), 5000);
}
```

This function sends parameters to the builder and it generates a new notification. If you want to know all the properties, go to https://developer.mozilla.org/en-US/docs/Web/API/notification.

191

Using Push Notifications in VueNoteApp

Now that we've taken a look at the principle APIs and the process for pushing notifications, let's add this feature to our app.

Configuring the App

In our Firebase project, select Project settings (Figure 8-3).

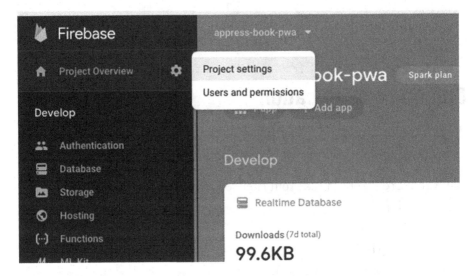

Figure 8-3. *Firebase project settings*

In Project settings, select Cloud Messaging (Figure 8-4). Note the server key and the sender ID for later use.

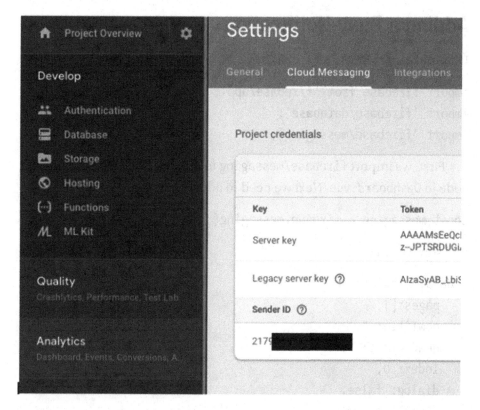

Figure 8-4. *Firebase Cloud Messaging*

Next we need to add gcm_sender_id, which is "103953800507" to all the apps in the world that use the Firebase service. We add this property to our manifest.json file:

```
"gcm_sender_id": "103953800507"
```

Okay. Now we are ready to use cloud messaging in VueNoteApp.

193

Adding a Push Notification

Let's add some values to firebase.js:

```
import firebase from 'firebase/app';
import 'firebase/database';
import 'firebase/messaging';
```

First, we import firebase/messaging to our app, then we add some code in Dashboard.vue. Next we need to add a constant

```
const messaging = fireApp.messaging();
```

and some extra data

```
data: () => ({
  pages:[],
  newTitle: ",
  newContent: ",
  index: 0,
  dialog: false,
  showAlert: false,
  alertContent: 'demo'
}),
```

We need showAlert and alertContent properties to handle when a notification is sent to our PWA.

Then we use retrieveMessaging() in Dashboard.vue to get the permission and the token to identify our device.

```
retrieveMessaging () {
  // Retrieve Firebase Messaging object.
  messaging.requestPermission()
```

```
.then(() => {
  //Notification permission granted.

messaging.getToken()
.then((currentToken) => {
  if (currentToken) {
    console.log("token:" + currentToken );
  } else {
    // Show permission request.
    console.log('No Instance ID token available. Request
    permission to generate one.');
  }
})
.catch((err) => {
  console.log('An error occurred while retrieving
  token. ', err);
});

this.onMessage();

})
.catch(function(err) {
  console.log('Unable to get permission to notify.', err);
});

}
```

We use the token later. We also need to use the onMessage() method to show our notification:

```
onMessage() {
  messaging.onMessage((payload) => {
    console.log("Message received. ", payload);
    this.showAlert = true;
```

```
        this.alertContent = payload.notification.body;
    });
  }
```

Here we show the notification and the text in our app. We also need to use the v-alert component in the template. You can find more information at https://vuetifyjs.com/es-MX/components/alerts.

```
<v-alert
      v-model="showAlert"
      type="info"
      dismissible
    >
      {{alertContent}}
</v-alert>
```

Then we add retrieveMessaging() in the mounted() life cycle hook:

```
mounted() {
  db.once('value', (notes) => {
    notes.forEach((note) => {
      this.pages.push({
        title: note.child('title').val(),
        content: note.child('content').val(),
        ref: note.ref
      })
    })
  });

  this.retrieveMessaging();
},
```

The next thing we need to do is create a service worker that handles messages in the background. To do this, we need to make a firebase-messaging-sw.js file (which is the name to use if you are going to use the Firebase library) at the same level as index.html. In index.html, we implement push notification handling. To do this, we need to modify some files.

vue.config.js

```
module.exports = {
    pwa: {
        // Configure the Workbox plug-in.
        workboxPluginMode: 'InjectManifest',
        workboxOptions: {
            // swSrc is required in InjectManifest mode.
            swSrc: 'src/firebase-messaging-sw.js',
        }
    }
}
```

In src/registerServiceWorker.js:

```
/* eslint-disable no-console */

import { register } from 'register-service-worker'

if (process.env.NODE_ENV === 'production') {
  register(`${process.env.BASE_URL}firebase-messaging-sw.js`, {
    ready () {
      /* console.log(
        'App is being served from cache by a service worker.\n' +
        'For more details, visit https://goo.gl/AFskqB'
      ); */
    },
```

```
  registered () {
    // console.log('Service worker has been registered.')
  },
  cached () {
    // console.log('Content has been cached for offline
    use.')
  },
  updatefound () {
    // console.log('New content is downloading.')
  },
  updated () {
    // console.log('New content is available; please
    refresh.')
  },
  offline () {
    // console.log('No Internet connection found. App is
    running in offline mode.')
  },
  error (error) {
    console.error('Error during service worker
    registration:', error)
  }
  })
}
```

Now we need to create a new `firebase-messaging-sw.js` file:

```
self.__precacheManifest = [].concat(self.__precacheManifest || []);
workbox.precaching.suppressWarnings();
workbox.precaching.precacheAndRoute(self.__precacheManifest, {});
importScripts('https://www.gstatic.com/firebasejs/5.5.6/
firebase-app.js');
```

```
importScripts('https://www.gstatic.com/firebasejs/5.5.6/
firebase-messaging.js');

firebase.initializeApp({
    'messagingSenderId': '217988350403'
 });

const messaging = firebase.messaging();

messaging.setBackgroundMessageHandler(function(payload) {
  console.log('[firebase-messaging-sw.js] Received background
  message ', payload);
  // Customize notification here.
  var notificationTitle = 'Background Message Title';
  var notificationOptions = {
    body: 'Background Message body.',
    icon: '/icons/icon-128x128.png'
  };

  return self.registration.showNotification(notificationTitle,
    notificationOptions);
});
```

With this code, we have added the Workbox offline features and the Firebase messaging background features to our app. Also, note that we are using senderId in the firebase.initializeApp() method.

Running the App

Okay. Now we need to run

```
$npm run build
```

```
$serve -s dist
```

Go to `http://localhost:5000`. You should see something similar to what is shown in Figure 8-5.

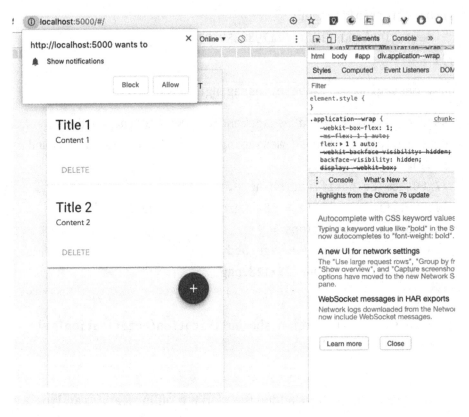

Figure 8-5. *Ask for permission in VueNoteApp*

After we allow notifications, the user token for this device shows up (Figure 8-6).

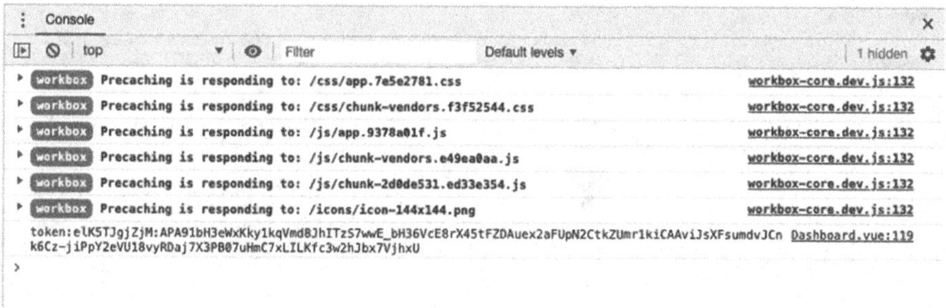

Figure 8-6. *Device ID token*

The thing here is that we need a server to send us push notifications, but we can fake this with a curl script. To test that the information is being sent from the terminal (in my case, I use a Mac), you can simulate a message with the following command:

```bash
#!/bin/bash
curl https://fcm.googleapis.com/fcm/send \
     -H "Content-Type: application/json" \
     -H "Authorization: key=XXXXX" \
     -d '{ "notification": {"title": "Push", "body":
     "This is a Foreground message.", "click_action" :
     "https://www.localhost.com"},"to" : "YYYYYY"}'
```

We simply have to change XXXXX using the server configuration key we found in the Cloud Messaging tab in the Project settings of our project in Firebase. We must also change YYYYYY using the user's token. We get the user's token from the page console.log. Now, every time we execute the script, we send a push notification to that client (Figure 8-7).

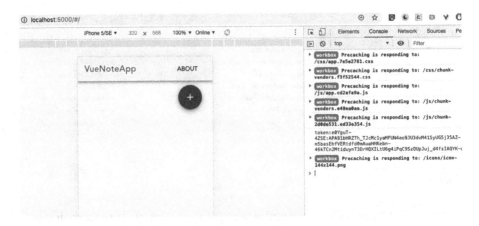

Figure 8-7. *Getting a message in VueNoteApp*

Figure 8-8 shows the notifications in the app.

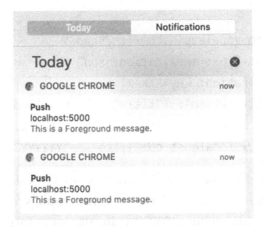

Figure 8-8. *Getting a push notification in VueNoteApp*

In the future, the push notification must be sent by a back-end server, but we are already handling the push service protocol and the notification.

You can go there from the repo (`https://github.com/carlosrojaso/appress-book-pwa`) with

```
$git checkout PushNotifications
```

If you are using a Mac, you can find `test.push.sh` script to make it more easy to simulate a push notification. Update with your server key and user token information and run

```
$./test.push.sh
```

Summary

Having push notifications allows us to interact with our users even when they have closed our app. In this chapter, we used various methods to generate a notification permission and to allow push notifications to appear in our PWA.

CHAPTER 9

Publishing

Congratulations! We have now our web app with an app icon, manifest, and service worker, which means our PWA can be installed, it works offline, and it supports push notifications. Now we need to share our app with the world. To do this, we need to send it to a web server with an SSL (a requirement for PWAs). Fortunately, Firebase Hosting can help us do this. In this chapter, we add a basic authentication system that allows users to have their accounts, thanks to the power of Firebase authentication.

Adding Firebase Authentication

Firebase gives us an easy way to add authentication to our JS app through its software development kit. We need to choose the sign-in providers that we will support in our app. We can choose between the most popular, Facebook and Google, until we integrate with our custom authentication system. Let's use an e-mail address and a password to keep things simple.

First, we go to go to the Firebase web console and select Authentication (Figure 9-1).

© Carlos Rojas 2020
C. Rojas, *Building Progressive Web Applications with Vue.js*,
https://doi.org/10.1007/978-1-4842-5334-2_9

Figure 9-1. Firebase authentication in the Firebase Web Console

In Authentication, we select "Sign-in method" (Figure 9-2).

Authentication

| Users | Sign-in method | Templates | Usage |

Sign-in providers

Figure 9-2. Sign-in method

Next, we enable Email/Password (Figure 9-3).

Email/Password

Enable

Allow users to sign up using their email address and password. Our SDKs also provide email
address verification, password recovery, and email address change primitives. Learn more

Email link (passwordless sign-in)   Enable

Cancel   Save

*Figure 9-3. Enabling email/password authentication in the Firebase
Web Console*

Okay. That's all in the web console for now. Back to our code. We need a new component with a form where we can enter an e-mail address and password, and generate the authentication process. Create the new file components/Login.vue.

Login.vue

```
<template>
  <div class="flex-container">
    <div class="row">
    <v-card>
    <v-toolbar
      card
      color="cyan"
      dark
    >
      <v-toolbar-title>{{actionText}}</v-toolbar-title>
    </v-toolbar>
    <v-form>
      <v-text-field
        v-model="email"
        :error-messages="emailErrors"
        label="E-mail"
        class="flex-item"
        required
        @input="$v.email.$touch()"
        @blur="$v.email.$touch()"
      ></v-text-field>
      <v-text-field
        v-model="password"
        class="flex-item"
        :append-icon="show1 ? 'visibility' : 'visibility_off'"
        :rules="[rules.required, rules.min]"
```

```
          :type="show1 ? 'text' : 'password'"
          label="Password"
          hint="At least 8 characters"
          counter
          @click:append="show1 = !show1"
        ></v-text-field>
        <div class="flex-item">
        <v-btn flat small v-if="actionButton==='Send'"
        @click="goToRegister()" color="primary">Register</v-btn>
        <v-btn flat small v-if="actionButton==='Register'"
        @click="goToLogin()" color="primary">Sign In</v-btn>
        </div>
        <div class="flex-item">
        <v-btn @click="submitAction()">{{actionButton}}</v-btn>
        <v-btn @click="clear">clear</v-btn>
        </div>
      </v-form>
      </v-card>
      </div>
    </div>
</template>

<script>
  import { validationMixin } from 'vuelidate';
  import { required, email } from 'vuelidate/lib/validators';
  import { fireApp } from '../firebase';

  const auth = fireApp.auth();

  export default {
    name: 'Login',
    mixins: [validationMixin],
```

```
validations: {
  email: { required, email },
},

data: () => ({
  actionText: 'Login',
  actionButton: 'Send',
  email: ",
  user: null,
  show1: false,
  password: 'Password',
  rules: {
      required: value => !!value || 'Required.',
      min: v => v.length >= 8 || 'Min 8 characters',
      emailMatch: () => ('The email and password you
      entered don\'t match')
    }
}),

mounted () {
  this.isUserLoggedIn()
  .then(()=> {
    this.goToDashboard();
    this.$root.$emit('USER_LOGGED',true);
  })
  .catch(()=> {})
  ;
},

computed: {
  emailErrors () {
    const errors = []
    if (!this.$v.email.$dirty) return errors
```

```
      !this.$v.email.email && errors.push('Must be valid
      e-mail')
      !this.$v.email.required && errors.push('E-mail is
      required')
      return errors
  }
},

methods: {
  submit () {
    this.$v.$touch()
  },
  isUserLoggedIn () {
    return new Promise(
      (resolve, reject) => {
        auth.onAuthStateChanged(function(user) {
          if (user) {
            this.user = user;
            resolve(user);
          }
          else {
            reject(user);
          }
        })
      }
    )
    ;
  },
  clear () {
    this.$v.$reset()
    this.name = "
    this.email = "
  },
```

```
goToLogin () {
  this.actionText= 'Login';
  this.actionButton= 'Send';
},
goToRegister () {
  this.actionText= 'Register';
  this.actionButton= 'Register';
},
goToDashboard () {
  this.$router.push('/dashboard');
},
signInUser (email, password) {
  auth.signInWithEmailAndPassword(email,password)
  .then(
    () => {
    this.goToDashboard();
    }
  )
  .catch(
    // eslint-disable-next-line
    (error) => {console.log('Something happened.', error)}
  );
},
signUpUser (email, password) {
  auth.createUserWithEmailAndPassword(email,password)
  .then(
    // eslint-disable-next-line
    (user) => {console.log('User registered.', user)}
  )
```

```
        .catch(
          // eslint-disable-next-line
          (error) => {console.log('Something happened.', error)}
        );
      },
      submitAction () {
        switch(this.actionText) {
        case 'Login':
          this.signInUser (this.email, this.password);
          break;
        case 'Register':
          this.signUpUser (this.email, this.password);
          break;
        }
      }
    }
  }
</script>
<!-- Add "scoped" attribute to limit CSS to this component only -->
<style scoped>
html, body {
    height: 100%;
}
body {
    margin: 0;
}

.flex-container {
    height: 100%;
    padding: 0;
    margin: 0;
```

```
        display: -webkit-box;
        display: -moz-box;
        display: -ms-flexbox;
        display: -webkit-flex;
        display: flex;
        align-items: center;
        justify-content: center;
    }

    .row {
        width: 95%;
    }
    .flex-item {
        width: 90%;
        margin: 5%;
        text-align: center;
    }
    }
</style>
```

With this code, we created a form with some validations using vuelidate. For more information, go to `https://github.com/vuelidate/vuelidate`. We install this dependency by running

```
$ npm install vuelidate --save
```

Then we use the method `submitAction()` to run `signInUser()` or `signUpUser()`, depending on the property `actionText`. This is because we are using the same component to authenticate and register users, and `actionText` is a flag that we use when users want to register or sign in to the app. With these methods, we use `createUserWithEmailAndPassword()` and `signInWithEmailAndPassword()` from the Firebase JS software development kit, which allows Firebase to handle this complexity for us.

For more information, go to https://firebase.google.com/docs/
reference/js/firebase.auth.Auth.html#createuserwithemailandpass
word and https://firebase.google.com/docs/reference/js/firebase.
auth.Auth.html#signinwithemailandpassword.

Another thing we need to take care of is, if users are logged in to our
app, they don't have to enter their user name and password again. To do
this, we use isUserLoggedIn(), which returns a promise when a user is
logged in already. If the user is logged in, we send to the dashboard and
emit an event to communicate to the header in our app that the user is
logged in, then show the logout option:

```
this.$root.$emit('USER_LOGGED',true);
```

this.$root is a way to use the root reference as a mechanism for
sharing information between components. When it is something as simple
as this value, this choice makes sense. However, if sharing information is
complicated, Vue.js has more sophisticated ways of doing this:

```
https://vuejs.org/v2/guide/mixins.html
```

Next we modify routes.js to add this new component.

routes.js

```
import Dashboard from './components/Dashboard.vue'
import Login from './components/Login.vue'
const lazyAbout = () => import('./components/About.vue')

export const routes = [
  {path: ", component: Login},
  {path: '/login', component: Login},
  {path: '/dashboard', component: Dashboard},
  {path: '/about', component: lazyAbout}
];
```

Figure 9-4 shows the results.

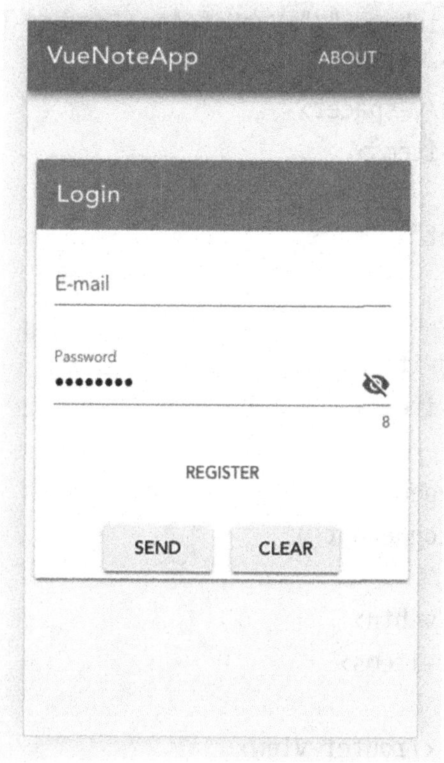

Figure 9-4. *Login component*

Now we need to add the logout link in App.vue.

App.vue

```
<template>
  <v-app>
    <v-toolbar
    color="light-blue"
    dark
```

```
    app>
      <v-toolbar-title>
        <router-link to="/">VueNoteApp</router-link>
      </v-toolbar-title>
      <v-spacer></v-spacer>
      <v-toolbar-items>
        <v-btn
        to="/about"
        flat
        >About</v-btn>
      </v-toolbar-items>
      <v-toolbar-items>
        <v-btn
        v-if="logged"
        @click="loggedOut()"
        flat
        >Logout</v-btn>
      </v-toolbar-items>
    </v-toolbar>
    <router-view></router-view>
  </v-app>
</template>

<script>
import { fireApp } from './firebase';

const auth = fireApp.auth();

export default {
  name: 'app',
  data: () => ({
    logged: false,
  }),
```

```
  mounted() {
    this.$root.$on('USER_LOGGED', (payload)=>{ this.logged =
    payload });
  },
  methods: {
    loggedOut () {
      auth.signOut()
      .then(()=>{
        this.$router.push('/login');
        this.logged= false;
        })
      .catch((error)=> {
        // eslint-disable-next-line
        console.log('error', error)
      })
      ;
    },
  }
}
</script>

<style>
#app {
  font-family: 'Avenir', Helvetica, Arial, sans-serif;
  -webkit-font-smoothing: antialiased;
  -moz-osx-font-smoothing: grayscale;
}

a, a:visited {
  text-decoration: none;
  color: white;
}
</style>
```

Next, we listen to this.$root to see if the user is logged in, then shows up, the logout link (Figure 9-5).

Figure 9-5. *User logged in, showing logout link*

And now we update Dashboard.vue to handle our authentication and get only those notes for each user using their ID.

```
<template>
  <div class="dashboard">
    <v-content>
      <Notes :pages="pages" @new-note="newNote" @delete-
      note="deleteNote"/>
    </v-content>
```

```
    <v-dialog v-model="dialog">
        <v-card>
        <v-card-title>
            <span class="headline">New Note</span>
        </v-card-title>
        <v-card-text>
            <v-container grid-list-md>
            <v-layout wrap>
                <v-flex xs12 sm12 md12>
                <v-text-field v-model="newTitle" value=""
                label="Title*" required></v-text-field>
                </v-flex>
                <v-flex xs12 sm12 md12>
                <v-textarea v-model="newContent" value=""
                label="Content"></v-textarea>
                </v-flex>
            </v-layout>
            </v-container>
            <small>*indicates required field</small>
        </v-card-text>
        <v-card-actions>
            <v-spacer></v-spacer>
            <v-btn color="blue darken-1" flat
            @click="closeModal()">Close</v-btn>
            <v-btn color="blue darken-1" flat
            @click="saveNote()">Save</v-btn>
        </v-card-actions>
        </v-card>
    </v-dialog>
  </div>
</template>
```

```
<script>
import {fireApp} from'../firebase.js'
import Notes from './Notes.vue'

const db = fireApp.database().ref();
const auth = fireApp.auth();

export default {
  name: 'Dashboard',
  components: {
    Notes
  },
  data: () => ({
    user: null,
    pages:[],
    newTitle: ",
    newContent: ",
    index: 0,
    dialog: false
  }),
  computed: {
  },
  mounted() {
    this.isUserLoggedIn()
    .then(
      (user) => {
        this.user = user;
        this.$root.$emit('USER_LOGGED',true);
        this.getUserNotes();
      }
    )
```

```
      .catch(
        () => {
          this.$router.push('/login');
        }
      )
      ;
},
methods:  {
  newNote () {
    this.dialog = true;
  },
  saveNote () {
    const newItem = {
      title: this.newTitle,
      content: this.newContent,
      userId: this.user.uid
    };
    this.pages.push(newItem);
    this.index = this.pages.length - 1;
    db.push(newItem);
    this.resetForm();
    this.closeModal();
  },
  closeModal () {
    this.dialog = false;
  },
  getUserNotes () {
    db.orderByChild('userId').equalTo(this.user.uid).
    once("value")
```

```
      .then(
        (notes) => {
          notes.forEach((note) => {
            this.pages.push({
              title: note.child('title').val(),
              content: note.child('content').val(),
              ref: note.ref
            })
          })
        }
      )
      .catch(
        (error) => {
          // eslint-disable-next-line
          console.log('something wrong happened!', error);
        }
      )
      ;
    },
    deleteNote (item) {
      let noteRef = this.pages[item].ref;
      if(noteRef) { noteRef.remove(); }
      this.pages.splice( item, 1);
      this.index = Math.max(this.index - 1, 0);
    },
    resetForm () {
      this.newTitle = ";
      this.newContent = ";
    },
```

```
isUserLoggedIn () {
    return new Promise(
        (resolve, reject) => {
            auth.onAuthStateChanged(function(user) {
                if (user) {
                    resolve(user);
                }
                else {
                    reject(user);
                }
            })
        }
    )
    ;
    },
  }
}
</script>

<!-- Add "scoped" attribute to limit CSS to this component only
-->
<style scoped>

</style>
```

In the previous code, we used getUserNotes() to get the notes associated with one user using the user ID db.orderByChild('userId'). equalTo(this.user.uid).once("value").

Now we need to go back to the Firebase web console and update our security rules (Figure 9-6).

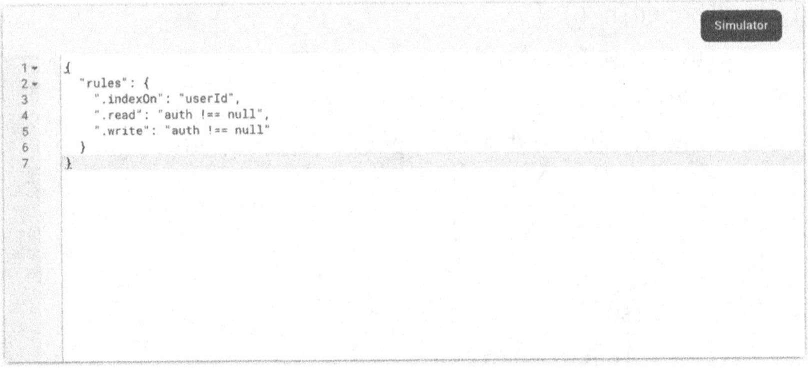

Figure 9-6. *Firebase Web console database security rules*

Now only logged-in sessions can read and write data in our database.

You can go there from the repo (`https://github.com/carlosrojaso/appress-book-pwa`) with

```
$git checkout v1.1.6
$npm run build
$serve -S dist
```

Sending to Firebase Hosting

Next we need to authenticate our Firebase CLI with our Firebase account. To do this, run

```
$ firebase login
```

After you achieve a successful authentication, we use the Firebase tool to connect our app with Firebase.

The next step is to create our production bundle. Run

```
$ npm run build
```

This creates the `dist/` folder with our optimized PWA. Now we need to run the Firebase CLI wizard to connect VueNoteApp with Firebase. Run the following and you should see what is pictured in Figure 9-7:

```
$ firebase init
```

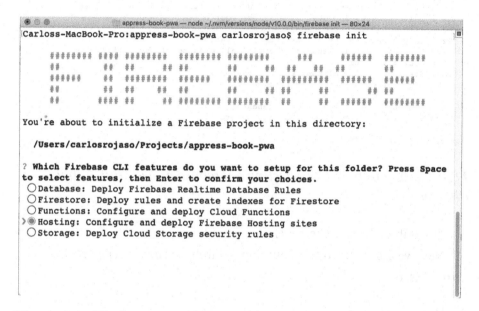

Figure 9-7. *Firebase CLI select service to configure*

Select Hosting and you should see what is displayed in Figure 9-8.

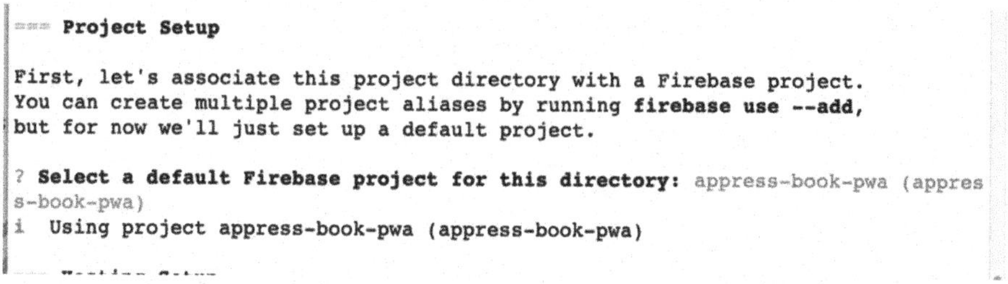

Figure 9-8. *Firebase CLI select Firebase project*

Select the project you created in https://firebase.google.com/—in my, case, appress-book-pwa, as shown in Figure 9-9.

```
=== Hosting Setup

Your public directory is the folder (relative to your project directory) that
will contain Hosting assets to be uploaded with firebase deploy. If you
have a build process for your assets, use your build's output directory.

? What do you want to use as your public directory? dist
? Configure as a single-page app (rewrite all urls to /index.html)? No
✔ Wrote dist/404.html
? File dist/index.html already exists. Overwrite? No
i Skipping write of dist/index.html

i Writing configuration info to firebase.json...
i Writing project information to .firebaserc...

✔ Firebase initialization complete!
```

Figure 9-9. *Firebase CLI selecting a Firebase project and public directory*

The public directory is dist/.

Now we are ready to send our app to Firebase Hosting (Figure 9-10). To do this, run

```
$ firebase deploy
```

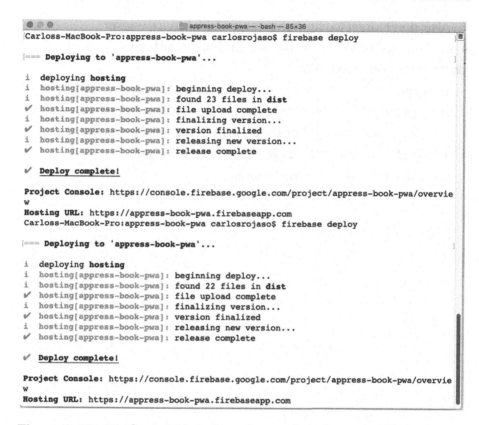

Figure 9-10. *Firebase CLI deployment and getting a public URL*

At the end, you get a hosting URL. This is your web URL. Try it now with `https://appress-book-pwa.firebaseapp.com`.

Final Thoughts

If you have reached this point, I congratulate you! You are now capable of implementing the basic features of a PWA in any existing web app. If you have any comments or feedback, don't hesitate to contact me at iam@carlosrojas.dev.

Also, don't forget to check the status of the service worker in the browsers in the "Can I Use" site (`https://caniuse.com/#search=service%20worker`).

If you find something in the code, don't hesitate to create an issue at `https://github.com/carlosrojaso/appress-book-pwa/issues`.

Last, make sure you update the code from the official repository: `https://github.com/carlosrojaso/appress-book-pwa`.

See you later and keep programming!

Index

S, T, U

Printed in the United States
By Bookmasters